The American Utopian Adventure

LETTERS FROM BROOK FARM, 1841-1847

ANNA Q. T. PARSONS

To whom many of the letters were written.

LETTERS FROM BROOK FARM
1844–1847

BY

MARIANNE (DWIGHT) ORVIS

EDITED BY

AMY L. REED

WITH A NOTE ON ANNA Q. T. PARSONS

BY HELEN DWIGHT ORVIS

PORCUPINE PRESS INC.

Philadelphia 1972

Library of Congress Cataloging in Publication Data

Orvis, Marianne (Dwight) 1818-1901.
Letters from Brook Farm, 1844-1847.

(The American utopian adventure)
1. Brook Farm. I. Title.
HX656.B807 1972 335'.9'74461 71-187455
ISBN 0-87991-011-9

First edition 1928 (Poughkeepsie, New York: Vassar College, 1928)

Reprinted 1972 by Porcupine Press, Inc., 1317 Filbert St., Philadelphia, Pa. 19107

Manufactured in the United States of America

CONTENTS

ILLUSTRATIONS

Originals in the possession of
Helen Dwight Orvis

INTRODUCTION

THESE letters of Mary Ann, or Marianne, Dwight are, I believe, the only considerable body of letters now in existence which were written on the spot by a member of the Brook Farm Community with the definite intention of describing the life of the place. They are the property of Miss Helen Dwight Orvis, of Wellesley, Massachusetts, the daughter of the writer, who gives them to print in the hope that they may help Americans of the present generation to realize how interesting it was to live in that oasis in the desert of competitive, industrial civilization.

Dissatisfaction with Main Street is no new thing. The contrast between the agricultural democracy seen in vision by the patriots of 1776 and the industrial republic actually inhabited by Americans in the second quarter of the nineteenth century filled many a thoughtful citizen of that latter day with profound misgiving. Emerson's call to a new way of life in the *American Scholar* in 1837 made so great a stir because his sweeping indictment of contemporary civilization was felt to be true. "The mind of this country," he said, "taught to aim at low objects, eats upon itself. . . . Young men of the fairest promise, who begin life upon our shores, inflated by the mountain winds, shined upon by all the stars of God, find the earth below not in unison with these, but are hindered from action by the disgust which the principles on which business is managed inspire, and turn drudges, or die of disgust, some of them suicides." Brook Farm, founded in 1841 on the "associative," or coöperative, principle in industry, was intended as a city of refuge for men and women who refused to be absorbed by money making.

But that is only one half of the story, the negative half. Brook Farmers had also a social purpose — to find a way of life that should be intellectually free and really interesting. Not until I read these letters did I realize how fully they succeeded in that aim. Surely Mary Ann Dwight had a good time! The combination in her letters of the details of her everyday occupations with the discussion of ideas has made plainer to me than any of the "recollections" of Brook Farm which I have read, what were the enjoyable elements in that unique society. The free and equal mingling of men and women, most of them young or in the prime of life, the presence of children of all ages, the combination of work and play, the satisfaction of the love of nature and of the art sense, the coming and going of distinguished visitors, the constant touch with the best thought of the outside world, the frequent "parties," the country walks, the conversation in congenial groups, — what wonder that, after having experienced all these and after Brook Farm had ceased to be, Marianne Dwight and her husband could never become reconciled to the ordinary routine of "civilization"?

While these letters thus present Brook Farm somewhat more vividly than I, at least, have been able to picture it hitherto, they in no way contradict but rather confirm the late Lindsay Swift's analysis and conclusions in his *Brook Farm.* To that book, with its admirably full bibliography, readers are referred who wish to know more about the conditions and consequences of the experiment and the personalities mentioned. My own notes, which are often much indebted to Swift's volume, are intentionally as brief and as few as possible. Their sole purpose is to clear away any possible confusion in reading the letters. The absence of a note on a proper name means either that I know nothing about the person in question, or that I regard the allusion as sufficiently self-explanatory.

I have thought it no part of my work as editor to describe the personality of the writer, who seems to me to describe herself as we read on. And I have left to Miss Orvis's competent pen the delineation of the very significant person to whom the majority of the letters were written.

A word on the geography of the situation may not be amiss. Brook Farm lies on the outskirts of the village of West Roxbury — sometimes called "the street" in these letters — eight miles from the center of Boston. The Farmers walked or drove into Boston for concerts, lectures, and meetings held to further the cause of "Association." Or they walked to Dedham, four miles away, and "took the cars" (railroad). A sketch reproduced on the title page of John T. Codman's *Brook Farm* shows the farm in 1846. Its 200 acres, now the site of an orphan asylum, remain almost intact and the "lay of the land" is very much what it was then, but the beautiful Pine Woods, back of the Eyrie, have been cut down and the only one of the original buildings now standing is the Cottage.

To Miss Helen Dwight Orvis and her brother, Mr. Christel Orvis, whose household at Wellesley breathes a cheerful serenity befitting the children of Brook Farmers, I wish to extend my heartfelt thanks for the double privilege they have accorded me of numbering myself among their friends and of editing their mother's letters.

Amy Louise Reed

Vassar College,
Poughkeepsie, N. Y.

A NOTE ON ANNA Q. T. PARSONS

Many of these letters were written from Brook Farm by Marianne Dwight to her most intimate friend, Anna Q. T. Parsons of Boston. The two young women were in the habit of going together to hear all the great speakers of the day upon such vital questions as slavery, economic reform, the position of women, or religious and ethical subjects. After one of these lectures—which often occurred at night — they would sometimes stand at the street corner where their ways divided, in such earnest conversation about what they had heard that they lost all sense of time until they heard a clock strike twelve, when they flew to their homes.

Letters to such a friend take on almost the character of a journal. Apparently nothing of moment is omitted regarding their daily life, their hopes and fears and plans. Some readers may think that a good deal of the detail is either of too personal or too trivial a nature to print. But it has been thought best to include most of this material, because it does so fully reveal the actual spirit of the Brook Farmers, their devotion to hard, constant work, their anxieties, their earnestness, their aspirations.

Anna Parsons lived to a great age. Even at ninety-three, she retained her memory for the events of her early life, and was able to explain with accuracy any puzzling allusions in these letters. Often a question would call forth quite a long and illuminating reminiscence.

From her girlhood days she was always interested in progressive movements and, though prevented by frail health from taking the active parts she desired, she worked steadily and used her personal influence to further coöperative homes and stores, women's exchanges, and the cause of "Association." She wrote articles in the Harbinger and in Greeley's Tribune. She was one of the founders of the Boston Religious Union of Associationists, and its secretary, and she also founded the Boston Women's Associative Union.

A word is necessary in explanation of the frequent allusion made in this book to her reading of character by letters. This gift in her was of great interest to herself and to others who saw and heard her do it. The method was either to hold the letter in her hand without looking at it, or to put it against her forehead, and to give herself up to the psychic impressions then received. After a few minutes, she would begin to talk about the character of the writer, while some one present made notes. Less often, she would make the notes herself. This process was, however, a great tax upon her vitality, and her friends often urged her either not to "read" too often or to lay it aside altogether. She was so perfectly sincere a person, that, while people were surprised at the accuracy of her descriptions of character, no one ever questioned the genuineness of the process by which her impressions were obtained. As a specimen of this power, which so much interested such leaders of thought as George Ripley, Margaret Fuller, Emerson, and William Henry Channing, her reading of the character of Charles Fourier is given in the Appendix to this volume.

Miss Parsons was a frequent visitor at Brook Farm and some of her letters written from there are headed "Heaven." She longed to become a member but was prevented by family obligations. She was one of its most earnest well-wishers and to her "combined home" on Pinckney Street, a coöperative house run somewhat on Brook Farm principles, some of the people went after the Farm was given up. Here John Dwight and Mary Bullard were married and here Anna Parsons started her Union or Woman's Exchange.

The day before the sale of Brook Farm at auction was Fast Day and some of the young folk of the Religious Union had a picnic at Bussey Hill woods. William Henry Channing and Anna Parsons attended it, and then went on to Brook Farm to spend the night with Miss Macdaniel, who was living all alone at the Eyrie. She and the Codman family at the Hive were all that were left of the remarkable group who had formerly made their home there. In the evening, after a picnic supper to which all contributed, Mr. Channing read aloud, from a volume he had brought out in his pocket, Browning's new poem, *Paracelsus*. The next morning, when none of the party could bear to be present during the sale, they went into the Pine Woods, where Mr. Channing finished reading the poem and they spent the day on the spot so endeared to them, where their Sunday services had sometimes been held. After all was over and the people gone, they returned and all had supper with the Codmans at the Hive.

Some time before this when there had been talk of disbanding, Anna Parsons had said, "If Brook Farm is given up, I will go to its funeral," and Rebecca Codman added, "And I will stay behind and sweep it up." And this they literally did.

HELEN DWIGHT ORVIS

WELLESLEY, MASSACHUSETTS.
March, 1928.

Brook Farm, West Roxbury, Mass.
Thursday a.m., [Spring, 1844].

Dearest Anna,

Thanks, thanks for your note and all the interesting things you told me. . . . And now where do you think I am and what do you think I am about? In the *barn*, taking care of *three babies* about eighteen months old! The sun shines warm, the breeze is gentle and spring like, and fragrant with hay. It is one of the loveliest of spring days, — a day to be out of doors, and therefore I have chosen to fix the nursery for today in the open barn. This is my first entrance upon duty. For company, besides the babies, I have a goodly row of cows and oxen — a great, good natured dog, — occasionally a call from one and another, — and a parcel of little romping girls and boys who are keeping fast day as a holiday. I have had calls from Horace,[1] Fred Cabot,[2] Mr. Pratt,[3] Lucas,[4] Mr.

[1] Horace Sumner, brother of Charles Sumner.

[2] The manuscript records of Brook Farm in the library of the Massachusetts Historical Society show that seventy-three members of the Brook Farm Association for Industry and Education signed the revised constitution of 1844. There Mary Ann Dwight of Boston, born 1816, gives her occupation as that of a teacher. Frederick S. Cabot, of Boston, "clerk," was some six years younger. Anna Parsons was about three years older than Mary Ann (or Marianne) Dwight.

[3] Minot Pratt, the head farmer.

[4] The brothers, Lucas and José Corrales, young Spaniards from Manila, were pupils in the school.

Bradford,[1] who has just arrived, father,[2] John,[3] etc., etc., and many of the ladies. Fanny[4] has been doing the dormitory. But I must go back to the beginning and tell you all from our arrival. Our ride out was very pleasant, all the *bees*[5] were in the Hive at supper when the stage stopped, and our arrival created quite a sensation. John, Dana[6] and Horace waited on us in, Dora[7] and others welcomed us in the entry. We were ushered to the table where everything wore the same appearance of neatness and refinement I have always observed when I have been here. After supper we went, Mother to the Eyrie,[8] and Fanny and I to the Morton House[9] to inspect our apartment and put *to rights*. Thanks to the kind foresight of friends, we found our carpet spread out and our beds up. In my little room everything fits nicely. It is more roomy and convenient than I had an idea. They had placed the bed, bureaus, and washstand just where I wished, and soon we shall be in prime order, — didn't do much to the room on that

[1] George P. Bradford, formerly a Unitarian clergyman.

[2] Dr. John Dwight's medical skill served the community well in more than one serious situation.

[3] John Sullivan Dwight, editor, teacher, and musical critic. His biography is by George Willis Cooke, Boston, 1898.

[4] Marianne's sister, Frances Ellen Dwight, was at this time twenty-five years old. She assisted her brother John in teaching music at Brook Farm.

[5] The Brook Farmers. The largest building was called the Hive.

[6] Charles A. Dana, later famous as editor of the New York Sun, was one of the original shareholders and always an influential member of the community. He taught Greek and German in the school. He was at this time twenty-five years old.

[7] Dora Wilder.

[8] The Eyrie, built on the highest point in the Farm, contained the school, the library, and pianos, as well as rooms for residence.

[9] The Morton House, named after its first owner, was presently rechristened the Pilgrim House.

first visit, but went over to the Eyrie to spend the evening, where we had flute and piano music. And oh! what a magnificent evening! Full moon light from the Eyrie parlor was splendid; everything glittered like pure white snow. Again and again I wished you and Helen [1] were here. Before nine o'clock Mr. and Mrs. Ripley [2] came home and gave us a cordial welcome. Dora came in and we had quite a nice talk together. Mrs. Ripley ran across the room to us and said to me, "I really envy you, you are having such a good talk; — Dora never finds time to talk to me, — has never had any talk with me since she came." I asked her to take my seat for a talk with Dora — "No, I won't, I'm so *offended*." Mrs. Ripley said we were tired and must rest several days, for if we once began to work, we should never think we could stop. She charged Fanny and me not to get up to breakfast the next morning, saying we should have our breakfast sent up to the house.

But the next — (I've forgotten something and must go back. Fanny and Horace walked into the Pine Woods in the evening moonlight, and described the scene as surpassingly beautiful. I was too tired to go with them.) The next morning we rose soon after six — Horace knocked at our chamber door, and waited upon us down to the Hive for breakfast. After this we went back and went to work putting our rooms in order. We were busied so nearly all day, when we were not sitting still to rest. My box of books is not yet opened — when I get it unpacked and all its contents arranged, our room will look very pleasant and homelike. Directly after dinner, Messrs. Ripley, Dana,

[1] Helen Parsons, sister of Anna.

[2] George Ripley and Sophia Willard (Dana) Ripley, the founders of Brook Farm.

Ryckman [1] and List [2] started for New York. Dana carried our regards to Cranch.[3] . . . Before leaving . . . Mr. Ripley told Fanny and me in a very amusing way, how "pleasant it was to him to see *Christian people* about (alluding to us) and *proper*, *grown up*, well *behaved* young women, free from all the vices of the *world*, and *filled with all the virtues of association*." In the afternoon came the rest of our furniture (except what didn't) and the piano-forte, and about tea time came father. He said the supper reminded him of college commons, except that there were ladies present. Father is pleased with the place, and we are all thus far pleased and happy. I must own to one little *twinge of heart*.

Marianne

Thursday eve.

Have been in the refectory — had a grand time setting table. Mary Ann R.[4] said it was set uncommonly well. After tea washed *all* the cups and saucers, Fred C. wiped them — Had a *grand* time — To night will be a meeting in our parlor for rustic amusements — and tomorrow morning, what think you, I am *to wait on the table.*

Mary Ann

Thursday p.m. [*1844*].

And now, dearest Anna, I am *at home* in our own little home in a corner of the Pilgrim House, so I will finish

[1] Lewis K. Ryckman, a cordwainer.

[2] Christopher List.

[3] The poet and artist, Christopher Pearse Cranch, a close friend of John S. Dwight, was a frequent visitor at the Farm, where his singing and playing gave much pleasure.

[4] Marianne, or Mary Ann, Ripley, sister of George Ripley, headed the primary department of the school and was in charge of the Nest, a small building across the road from the entrance to Brook Farm. Her advice was always influential with her brother.

writing to you. . . . I was owning to one twinge of heart, — it was when Mrs. Ripley asked me if I would be willing to be in the nursery from eight o'clock till twelve. I told her I would try, but said I didn't think I should like it, or understand the management. However, I did very well this morning, — believe I am to have some older children with them hereafter, which will make it pleasanter. Today the babies were all asleep by eleven o'clock, so I sent them into the house, and had a little leisure to continue writing to you. This afternoon father has put up my book-shelves, and I have been unpacking and arranging books whilst Frances has been over to the Cottage to sing with the singing class. John is their teacher. Oh! that young Kay![1] I would I could draw his portrait. He is a character, be assured. . . . Dora and Martin Cushing went to Hingham yesterday to return this p.m. Dora and I were speaking together yesterday, when along came Mrs. Ripley. "At it again," said she, "Dora has not given me five minutes since she came to the community," — and off she walked with a very mock-resentful air. I have this afternoon received a few lines from Mrs. Ripley asking if I would join the refectory from half an hour before tea to an hour and a half after tea, as some of the group are desirous that I should. This is but a temporary arrangement during someone's absence, if I would like. I returned for answer, "yes." I feel as tho' I should like to go into all or almost all the departments for a little while, to see how everything is managed. Fred Cabot is as busy as a bee; — says he wants to have a talk with me about that letter of A. P.[2] when we can get a chance. Horace, who is our neighbor,[3]

[1] James Alfred, or "Allie," Kay, one of the pupils in the school.

[2] Anna Parsons.

[3] *I.e.*, in the Pilgrim House.

leaves tomorrow for New Hampshire — I am more sorry than I can tell . . . Dora will be our neighbor soon — Miss Willard's door is very near — Mary Ann Ripley's too, and Miss Russell [1] will soon be within two or three doors. I think I may say our room is really pretty and convenient and looks like home, and thus far we feel at home in it. Mother has just made me a call, — says she and father feel at home. Oh, my dear, good Anna ! the tears *will* come when I think of being thus separated from you. Tho' I came here with so little apparent emotion, yet I have deep feeling about this change ; so deep that I feel pretty sure it has not wholly revealed itself even to me, but will keep welling up from time to time. You and yours are to me all Boston, — *are more* than all Boston. Were you here, I do believe I should be entirely happy, — I mean as happy as it is in my nature to be whilst on this unbeautified and ill treated earth. Well, I write you truly, I am not homesick, but it distresses me so to think that I am obliged to resort to pen and ink to communicate my thoughts to you, that I shall not venture again immediately to speak on this subject — Fanny will ask what I am crying about.[2] . . . My love to Lucy Goddard. It would have delighted me to have been at her house that p.m. Did you have a good time and some good readings ? [3] Do tell me about them. How I long to have you and Helen [4] come out here now, and see us, and see how comfortable and happy we seem, in spite of the necessary shortcomings of the *actual*. I shall try (and

[1] Amelia Russell. See her two articles on the *Home Life of the Brook Farm Association* in Atlantic Monthly, 1878, v. 42, pp. 458–466, 556–563.

[2] Her sister, Fanny, occupies the same room.

[3] These readings are described in Miss Orvis's prefatory note on Anna Parsons.

[4] Helen Parsons.

you know I have a tact at it) to idealize the actual.[1] Do I not need your spiritual influence, amidst this mass of the material, which has not yet troubled me, but which I doubt not will be revealed bye and bye? Must I not, can I not have you here? My eleven cent goes to breakfast and thus far muslin de laine to dinner! Mud on the men's boots has not troubled me, — am much more troubled by that on my own india-rubbers! It will soon, I trust, be good walking. Birds sing and the country is delightful. . . . Do write as soon, as often and as long as you can, if you would be the best girl in the world. In haste. Off for the refectory.

Your friend
Mary Ann

Brook Farm, Sunday, April 14, '44.

Dear brother Frank,[2]

I did not mean it should be so long before you had a letter from me, but so many different things have taken up my time that I hardly know when I could have written. . . . I have taken a joyful leave of the nursery and the babies, — with one exception, the sweet little innocents were not to my taste, and not *such* angels as I love to minister to. Now my business is as follows (but perhaps liable to frequent change): I wait on the breakfast table (½ hour), help M. A. Ripley [3] clear away breakfast things, etc. (1½ hours), go into the dormitory group till eleven o'clock, — dress for dinner

[1] This attempt to "idealize the actual" is characteristic of the place and the period. We are reminded that Hawthorne always speaks of the manure pile which it was his task to transfer as "the gold mine." *American Note Books*, Riverside ed., pp. 233–35.

[2] Benjamin Franklin Dwight, Marianne's brother, was in an architect's office in Boston.

[3] Mary Ann Ripley.

— then over to the Eyrie and sew till dinner time, — half past twelve. Then from half past one or two o'clock until ½ past five, I teach drawing in Pilgrim Hall and sew in the Eyrie. At ½ past five go down to the Hive, to help set the tea table, and afterwards I wash tea cups, etc., till about ½ past seven. Thus I make out a long day of it, but alternation of work and pleasant company and chats make it pleasant. I am about entering a flower garden group[1] and assisting Miss Russell in doing up muslins. I have one very pleasant drawing class, consisting of the young ladies and the young men, José, Martin Cushing, etc. The other class is composed of the children in the regular school. We enjoy ourselves here very well, and I can't but think that after some weeks I shall become deeply attached to the place — I have felt perfectly at home from the first. We need more leisure, or rather, we should like it. There are so many, and so few women to do the work, that we have to be nearly all the time about it. I can't find time to write till it comes

[1] When the Dwight family joined the Brook Farm Association, the community was well on its way to become a Fourier phalanx on a much smaller scale. Fourier's organization of workers into "groups and series" according to their preference ("passional attraction") for certain kinds of work is elaborately explained in the Harbinger for Saturday, October 10, 1846, in an article on *Objections to Association;* more simply in Lindsay Swift's *Brook Farm*, pp. 44–45.

François Charles Marie Fourier (1772–1837), son of a French linen draper, wrote a number of socialistic books of which *Le nouveau Monde industriel*, 1829–30, contains the fullest exposition of his ideas. His system was based on the belief that the free play of strong individual desire was likely to bring about the most harmonious social living. Without advocating community of property or the abolition of the family, he planned the regrouping of society in "phalanxes" of about 1600 persons, living in large communal houses and subdivided into series and groups, working coöperatively under elective heads. The small numbers at Brook Farm prevented anything like the complete carrying out of Fourier's idea. But they did their best.

evening, and then we generally assemble in little bands somewhere for a little talk or amusement. Fred Cabot and Martin Cushing have moved into Horace's room, and I wish for the fun of it, you could look in and see how they have placed their beds, — across the door, so they are obliged to vault over them to get at what they call their parlor, which is by the window. They are full of fun and roguery. A day or two since, we looked in there and behold they had got our *images*, — cologne bottle, ink stand, etc., paraded out on their table. Martin is a good fellow, and makes a great deal of amusement for the whole house. He says he means to carry Fanny and me into Boston some Sunday. Oh! I love the Sundays here. This whole afternoon I have spent in the Pine Woods, and have wanted you here more than I can tell. We have much sickness here now, cases of scarlatina. Carry Pratt's [1] and Alfred Kay's are pretty severe cases, but all are now mending. Father came at the right time.

I really think you would enjoy living here, Frank, and hope that, if we stay, you will come. Come out that evening you have talked about when next we have full moon. . . . The Codmans [2] have come. The Campbells won't do, and are going away. I believe eight or ten more men are to come this next week. You can't think how we want to see you. . . . This evening in a few minutes will be a general gathering at the Hive to hear an account of the New York convention,[3] which I wish to attend. So must bid you good

[1] One of Minot Pratt's three children.

[2] The Codman family consisted of the parents, one daughter, Rebecca, and two sons, Charles H. and John T., the author of *Brook Farm: Historical and Personal Memoirs*, Boston, 1894.

[3] A socialist convention held at Clinton Hall, New York, George Ripley presiding. The meeting laid emphasis on the religious aspect of the socialist

bye now — will add a few words afterwards, if not too late. . . .

Your affectionate sister
Mary Ann

P.S. Mr. Ripley brought letters yesterday from you, Anna, and Helen.[1] We had quite a party in the evening in our little room.

Brook Farm, April 17, '44.

My dear friend Anna,

There are several things to which I would gladly devote the little leisure between the present time (quarter past one) and my drawing hour, which will be at two o'clock, but I choose to give it to you. . . . Dora seems quite cheerful and happy now. She has a pleasant little room all to herself, — the door opening close to the one occupied by Fred C.[2] and M. Cushing, as well as close to ours. We call the three rooms "our suite" of apartments and seem to feel a common family interest in them. Frederick and Martin have just moved out of a little room they had for a day or two, and taken Dora's, who has gone into the next, — and now I think we are nicely fixed for some time to come, — at least we don't expect any more moving for two or three months. We are quite neighborly. At half-past five in the morning comes a knock at our door; I call out "good-morning." Perhaps F. answers, "Good-morning, ma voisine, how are you today?" or Martin says, "Good-morning, how do you feel? and how does *our sister* do?" (meaning Fanny). Last evening Fred brought up a

movement and indorsed Fourier's principles of industrial organization. Frothingham, O. B., *Memoir of William Henry Channing*, p. 207.

[1] Helen Parsons.

[2] Fred Cabot.

large looking glass for their room, which he had begged of some new-comer, and as he and Martin both had to go to the Eyrie to watch with some sick folks, after his departure Dora and I took it up into her room and set it up. Fred, before leaving for the night, gave us a long and earnest lecture upon the absurdity and ridiculousness of ladies' wearing "*little fixings*," some hundred of which he, being in the washing department, had been compelled to hang out to dry. He began to be more definite at length, and explained that the little fixings meant *night-caps edged with lace!* (I had such a one in the wash; I presume he read my name on it.) He thinks it extremely absurd and injurious to wear night-caps. We combatted all his arguments and told him this morning that we looked at ourselves in night-caps last night in his beautiful glass, which Dora had appropriated, and the caps were never so becoming before.

Evening. The fancy I have had for Mr. List is clean gone forever. This evening, at tea time, we found stuck up on the wall of the dining hall a notice of the Association convention to be held in Parker's church[1] tomorrow. After tea in came List — asked Mr. Cabot if *he* put that up — was answered in the negative. Soon Mr. L. when no one saw him, took it down. All had gone but a few of the boys, Mrs. Ripley and we girls, who were washing the tea-cups. Fred gave him a severe trimming therefor, — wish you could have heard it — it was rich to us all. He said just the right thing in just the right way, and afterwards we each gave Fred a pin and he put it up again. When

[1] At West Roxbury. The reason for List's removing the notice may have been a feeling that the enthusiasm of the Brook Farmers over the recent socialist convention in New York threatened to carry them too far.

Mr. List came in again, Martin C. read it aloud. Mr. Cabot told List, that if he took it down again, it should be brought before the association. List took it down, and the boys put it up again, where it remained when I left the Hive. It is quite an affair. List is presumptuous and arrogant and very desirous of having the rule. I don't believe he will stay here long, — a few more such steps and his race will be run.

Last Sunday evening we had a meeting to hear Mr. Ripley's report of the New York convention. We are going to have Fourier meetings every Sunday evening. We are enjoying ourselves here very much. There are a great many things I would like to tell you, but I really have no time now. . . . Come and see us by the first moonlight, — let us have a grand evening together — write soon. . . . Farewell, dearest. How I long for you!

Your affectionate
Mary Ann

Brook Farm, Sat. a.m., April 27, 1844.

Dearest Anna,

I intended to have written you a full letter last evening, but we had company come in (up in our room), Fred C. and William Coleman, and were drawn into playing whist and talking till *eleven o'clock,* which in these working days, is as late an hour as I like to keep. Evening before last went into the Pine Woods about sunset, with Dora, Miss Codman, Fanny, Fred C. and one or two more. Oh! how sacred and solemn were those deep shades, and the sombre light! We threw ourselves upon our backs, Dora, Frederick and I, and whilst the rest walked on, and finally walked home, we staid (imprudent children) and talked till about nine o'clock when the dampness warned us home. How beautiful the moonbeams flickering through the leaves, as we gazed up into the sky, and here and there a star spangled the magically figured firmament above us! . . . Our earnest talk strengthened my faith in Association and in Brook Farm. — In which latter, strange to say, Dora's heart fails her. — But she will and must, I think, alter her mind. Oh! it is so pleasant here, even with all the work! I am sorry if Frank [1] carried you my last note, for I did not finish what I had begun to say and now forget about it. I believe I was going to tell you that, owing to Mary Ann Ripley's being ill two or three days, I had had more work to do than usual, as I endeavored in part, to supply her place. — Have you recovered your impressibility? [2] We had a gentleman here a few days ago, by name John Orvis,[3] who has lived at Skaneateles with Collins.[4] He is a very interesting and delightful young man, — is *very* impressible, reads characters thro' letters, or by coming in contact with a person. — Fred put him to sleep in a few moments, and also cured him of sore throat and head-ache, which complaints he had taken from Frances by relieving her of them. Frances proves to be rather impressible. Mr. Orvis did not undertake to examine any letters, in consequence of his head-ache, but read Abby Foord's character finely by putting his hand on

[1] Frank Dwight.

[2] *I.e.* her sensitiveness to impressions gained by holding to her forehead a letter or other paper written by the "subject" whose character was to be "read." See Miss Orvis's note on Anna Parsons.

[3] John Orvis, "farmer," Ferrisburgh, Vermont, about the same age as Mary Ann Dwight and destined to be of considerable importance in her life. He was already interested in Fourierism. Swift, *Brook Farm*, p. 278.

[4] John A. Collins, founder of the Skaneateles Community, which adopted Fourier's principles. Orvis was one of the signers of the call for the Association meeting at Skaneateles, March 22, 1843.

her head. — Well, the best of it is that he is coming here to live in two or three weeks, in consequence of being so much pleased with his visit, and he wants to be in *our entry* in Pilgrim Hall, and perhaps Fred will take him in with him if Martin leaves soon. Oh! how Mr. Kay[1] has teazed us about inveigling Mr. Orvis into our house! Then the Macdaniels[2] are to come this week and have one of our parlors. He insists upon it that the character of our house is to be changed, that the elegance and refinement of the place are tending this way. I tell him no—the Eyrie—the Eyrie! So has it been, and will ever be till we get our Phalanstery.[3]

The boys have brought us some anemones and cowslips, — wish I had some now to send. — But I write particularly to ask that when the rest of you come out here (I refer to the party by moonlight) you will by some means, bring little Fanny.[4] She can be tucked in anywhere and will not

[1] Mr. Kay, a New York business man, father of "Allie" Kay, was much interested in the success of Brook Farm. He was often called on for financial advice.

[2] The Macdaniels, mother, two daughters, Fanny and Eunice, and a son, Osborne, were a southern family. The son lived in New York, where he assisted Brisbane in editing the Phalanx. However, he visited the Farm frequently and for long periods.

[3] The Phalanstery, the central community house ("unitary building"), was begun in the summer of 1844. Hence the influx of carpenters. "All the public rooms were to be in this building, which was almost in the middle of the estate [of 200 acres]. The parlors, reading room, reception rooms, general assembly hall, dining room capable of seating over three hundred people, kitchen, and bakery were carefully planned for a common use." [There were also single rooms and suites for families.] The building was of wood and 175 feet long. Thus the larger families, whose members had been scattered by reason of the crowded condition of the other houses, could be insured a secluded family life, and such rooms in the older buildings as were in use for other than living purposes might be available for this legitimate need." Swift, *Brook Farm*, pp. 35-36.

[4] Anna Parsons's younger sister.

take up any room. A great deal of love to her, and tell her we shall be very much disappointed, if when your vehicles unpack at the Hive, she should not come to light. Love to all, — I am desirous of knowing what evening you will come; — will you send us word? perhaps Monday or Tuesday. — I don't know when the moon fulls, — but we are to have glorious evenings — Farewell.

Yours ever
Mary Ann

Brook Farm, half past five a.m., May 11, '44.

I wonder, dearest Anna, if I write with the speed of a race horse whether I can manage to tell you half that I have to say or even to fill out this sheet. I will try, but have my chamber to take care of before breakfast. It seems a long time since I have written to you or heard from you. Do believe that I will write always when I can, and when any cause occasions my notes to you to be few and far between, do let yours come to me often to cheer my labors or my loneliness, — for in spite of the good and lively companions about me, a feeling of loneliness does haunt me, when I can neither talk to you nor hear from you. I hope you will not take it into your head that you are not as needful to me now as ever, — there is no Anna Parsons here, no Helen, — no, none of that family, and I think I *must* go into Boston soon to make you all a call, and be again, for a short time, under your kindly influence; — I hunger and thirst for it, — hence my disappointment that the moon, after waiting in vain for you, has faded and passed away, without seeing you here. But you seem reconciled and don't regret not coming: But I am no stoic and I and *we* regret it every time we think of it. But that vanished moon has not gone forever, and perhaps her next visit will induce you to make us one. Oh! more and more beautiful every day is the prospect from our window. How rapidly, like magic, is the season advancing, — every dead-looking twig, bursting out with life and covering itself with beauty! Could such a change occur in the *moral* world, — in the dead hearts, the dry souls of men! And may we not hope that it will? that some new and hidden fount of life will be opened, that will gush out and revivify our whole existence? Yesterday I had a pleasant little walk, — gathered the rhodora in great abundance, and walked over beds of anemones. Our rocks are magnificent with columbine, — and our good boys keep our vases filled. I only wish for opportunities to send in flowers to you and other Boston friends. . . .

Sickness still continues here, and therefore we have additional work. Last Sunday night Lucas came near dying, — fortunately father was in the house to save him, and now he is pretty well. M. A. Ripley [1] is out again now, so I am released from my extra labors on her account. I am about making a change (that is I *think* of it) — leaving my refectory and dormitory work in the morning, and entering the consistory with Dora. She needs more help and I should like to become initiated in that business. — Dora has now a very bad cold — is usually in very good spirits — sometimes quite lively. The Macdaniels came from New York a day or two ago — think we shall like them very much. And now the time is about gone, and what shall I add? That we love Brook Farm more and more, — like its arrangements better and better, — and tho' we find fault (sometimes perhaps unreasonably) are patient with its imperfections and wait for the perfect day. Has your

[1] Mary Ann Ripley.

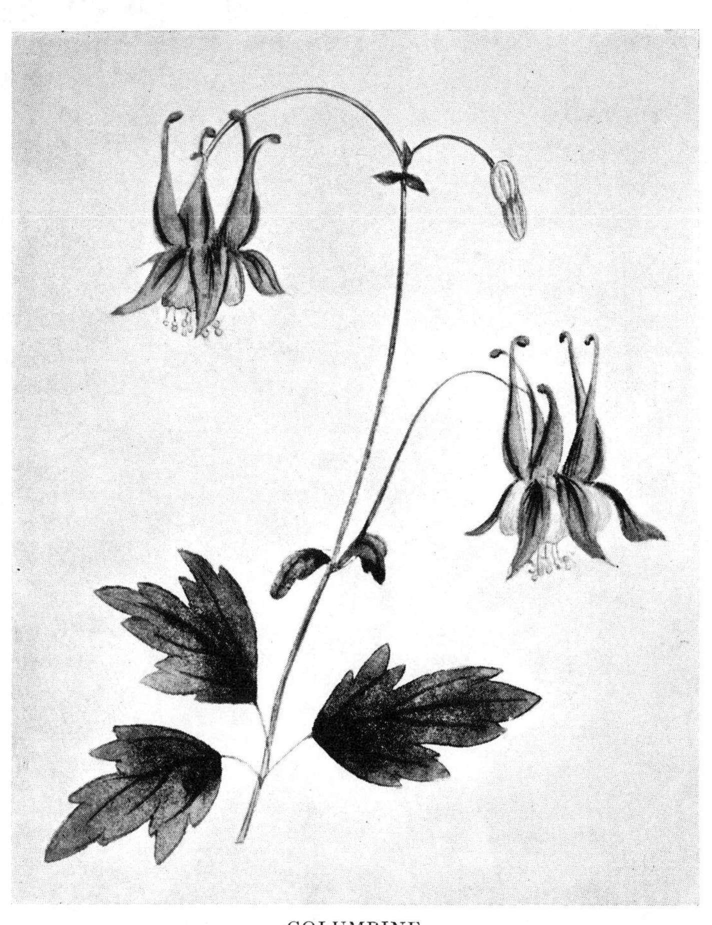

COLUMBINE

One of Marianne Dwight's many paintings.

impressibility returned? Don't forget to tell me. Mary Lincoln put a letter that I wrote her from Brook Farm into the hands of *Mr. Orvis*. Wasn't she a naughty child? . . . Give my love to Mary Bullard,[1] and tell her not to forget to come out here. . . .

Your dear friend
Mary Ann

Brook Farm, Wed. p.m., May 29, '44.

Dear Frank,

John Cheever is going to Boston tomorrow morning so I will send you a few words by him. . . . So many of our people came in to hear Ole Bull on Saturday evening that they thought the horse would be killed if they carried me out, so I stayed with Anna P. until Monday morning, when I took the Dedham cars. We all enjoyed the concert exceedingly; if you want to know how I feel about Ole Bull,[2] I will refer you to Mrs. Child's letter — the *last* letter. I hope you will hear him. He played the Carnival of Venice as an extra piece. He is an uncommonly fine looking man, his features, motions, attitudes, all expressive of genius. I enjoyed the concert the more for having seen Belshazzar's Feast,[3] which I carried there with me in my mind's eye. I was glad to receive your note from Mr. Dana, and to hear from Hingham. It was too bad that you had so dull a day. Dora and I have dissolved partnership in the consistory for a few days, in order that she may take Mr.

[1] A frequent visitor, who sang beautifully.

[2] Ole Bull, the Norwegian violinist, landed in Boston in November, 1843, and went directly to New York. Mrs. Child's letters, descriptions of the New York concerts, appeared in the *Boston Courier*. When he played in Boston in 1844, the Melodeon, a hall seating 2,000, was filled to overflowing.

[3] A painting by Washington Allston.

Reynolds' place in the kitchen during his absence. You may easily believe that I enjoyed my visit to Anna's very much — yet was truly glad to get home here — and right welcome and cheerful was the first glimpse I caught of the Eyrie, as I was walking from Dedham.

You must come out Saturday evening; we intend to entertain ourselves with tableaux, I believe, but I am quite at a loss to see how they will go off well, for Miss Russell is absent today and tomorrow, on account of the death of a friend, and she was to have had the arrangement. But come and see how well or how badly we shall do. . . . Fred Cabot is in Boston, — if you see him, remember me to him in a very friendly and sisterly manner. Tell him "our family" in Pilgrim Hall are prospering as well as we can without him. . . .

Your affectionate sister
Mary Ann

Brook Farm, June 4, '44.

Dearest Anna,

Our consistory work is finished, and I am going to take to myself the remainder of the forenoon, for the express purpose of writing to you. I sent in a little note to you Saturday, but behold it came back to me again in the evening, which was rather vexatious; — I sent it again to Miss Peabody's [1] yesterday, and trust it has reached its destination, — and now you must have a more full and complete account from me. I long to hear from you and learn if you all are well. I have not felt well since my visit to you. The damp weather makes my head-ache and

[1] Elizabeth Palmer Peabody, the distinguished educator. Her rooms in West Street housed her father's drug shop and a circulating library and were a convenient place of meeting or call for all the transcendental group.

lameness hold on, and the consistory labor is not very advantageous; — however, I dare say I shall be quite well soon. I wish you and your sisters had been here on Saturday evening, for the tableaux went off finely. — C. K. N.[1] honored us with his presence, and even praised my Jeanie Deanes and Winter performances as among the best. Of course I felt gratified, for I had great misgivings of myself, and little idea of being even tolerably successful. We wound up with the four seasons, — each making a different tableau. — 1st, Abby Foord and Pop[2] represented Spring; 2d, Charles Dana and Maria, Summer; 3d, Mr. Ripley and Fanny Macdaniel, Autumn; and 4th, Mr. Pratt and myself stood up as an aged couple, for Winter, with tremendous effect. I am assured, "They were excellent." For further description I refer you to a long letter that Frances has written to Frank. . . .

I forgot how much I wrote you about N. and the MS, but probably not all that I have to say. Did I tell you that I claimed *that page* for you in vain?[3] He said *no*, gently and

[1] These are the initials of Charles King Newcomb, poet, considered by all who knew him a very exceptional, finely organized, sensitive person. See George W. Curtis, *Early Letters to John S. Dwight*, p. 24, and Swift, *Brook Farm*, pp. 198–202. He was a boarder at the Farm, not a member of the Association, and held himself much aloof, "making a cult of contemplation."

[2] Short for Popleston.

[3] The explanation of this mysterious passage seems to be that Newcomb had written a poem which Mary Ann Dwight wished to borrow in order that Anna Parsons might "read" the young man's character by holding the paper to her forehead. She had already read some other MS of his, the notes of which (written down by Miss Dwight as the words came from Miss Parsons's lips) had been given to him and by him sent on to Miss Fuller. Apparently the "character" was beautiful enough to atone to him for the intrusion upon his sensitive soul.

Emerson greatly admired Newcomb's one contribution to the *Dial*, entitled *Dolon*.

softly, — but with a look and a meaning which made it *impossible* for me to try to persuade him. He says you know quite well enough what it contains. This is not want of simplicity, Anna, but the most entire naturalness. His delicate nature shrinks so from laying itself open to observation. He would not read nor show it to me, but said in answer to my interrogations that he was willing I should find it and read it, — that *perhaps* I might see it *sometime*, etc. (Dora gets interested in *all my pets:* — I no sooner fall to cherishing anybody than behold, our blessed Dora is at my side, a rival — But ours is not the evil rivalry which abounds in "the world," — but the true rivalry of Association: — we are *friends* and rivals: — we love each other the more for this kind of emulation.) N. tried to make me promise to destroy those notes, as soon as I had copied them legibly for him. — I told him "yes, if he wished it," — it was not in my power to say aught else, — but I finally persuaded him that it would be better I should keep them in a safe place, away from all eyes, until Margaret Fuller, to whom he has sent *his* copy, returns it. Still he says he thinks he shall destroy *that*, when it comes home to him. He gives me leave to read them over once more before I destroy them. Oh! it is too good and too beautiful and too true to destroy! I hope it will not be done. — Don't you recollect saying that the thoughts came to you so fast you could not possibly express them? Well, he says I must not tell of it (I said, to nobody but *you*), but Mr. Emerson said he never read anything of his but it filled him with many thoughts, — or never read anything that filled him with *so many* thoughts. Then he was struck with this remark of yours — that words came to you which would convey no idea to any one else, but which had a deep meaning to you — and he requested me to write that down. — Dora and I have more jokes with him than a few. You have no idea how we meet soul to soul in *fun*.

Are you going to hear Ole Bull to night? — I do hope that you will. How Fanny and I shall long to be there! — Mr. Butterfield, Rebecca Codman [1] and C. Newcomb are going, I believe. Mr. Westcot says he saw you at the Fourier meeting last eve. That was a grand meeting according to the account our people brought home. — They are in high spirits about it.

I thought to write you a long letter, but the dinner hour has surprised me, and I must give this to Mr. Butterfield at the table. . . .

Ever yours
Mary Ann

Brook Farm, July 6, '44.

Dear Frank,

Why don't we hear from you, and why did you not come out here on the 4th of July? Carry [2] leaves us within an hour, and we regret very much to part with her, having enjoyed her visit exceedingly. . . . Did you not get my note asking you to come out? We had a fine time, a pleasant dance in Pilgrim Hall — both parlors at our service — plenty of cherries, cake and lemonade. Wish you could have looked into Martin's room, and seen the great tub full of lemonade standing in the middle of it, as if all prepared for a bath. We had only three disappointments. You didn't come, Frank Cabot didn't come, and our fiddler didn't come. I should have time to write more to you now,

[1] Rebecca Codman later became the wife of Butterfield.

[2] "Cousin Carry Dwight." See letter of July 7, 1844.

but have spent my leisure with Carry, and the last part of it in taking a sketch for her which she may show you. What of the Parsonses? I long to write to Anna and will soon, so will I write to you — if tonight or tomorrow don't bring you. Dora is gone. Do write, do come. Adieu.

Your affectionate sister
Mary Ann

Will you lend Carry the Phalanx? [1]

Brook Farm, Sunday p.m., July 7, '44.

Dearest Anna,[2]

I rejoice that the silence between us is about to come to an end. I don't like any circumstances, however agreeable in other respects, which cruelly prevent my intercourse with you. . . . Oh! more than you will believe do I want you *here.* — Every day has its own history, — every quiet walk its own reflection and fancies, and every incident its peculiar interest, all of which I am ever longing to share with you. . . . In the midst of business and pleasures and pains, too, I have not unfrequently had a feeling of loneliness for want of a word with you . . . I have been haunted by a dismal vision of indefinite, unlimited space between us. — I will not undertake to enumerate all obstacles that have interfered with my writing, for they are very numerous. The last week I devoted all the leisure I could possibly obtain to

[1] "The Phalanx, or Journal of Social Science, devoted to the Cause of Association or Social Reform and the Elevation of the Human Race," published its first number on Thursday, Oct. 5, 1843, at the office of the Sun, New York. It was devoted to spreading Fourier's ideas. In 1845, it became "The Harbinger, devoted to Social and Political Progress. Published by the Brook Farm Phalanx."

[2] Since the letter of June 4, Anna Parsons had made a brief visit or call at Brook Farm.

cousin Carry Dwight, who has been making us a visit. She is very much pleased with Brook Farm, — longs to live here, and says that now she will have something to look forward to in case she can ever leave her home. . . .

Dora has been gone about a week and we need her very much, — but I don't believe any one misses her so much as I (unless it be John Cheever) for I always depended upon her, and consulted her, and you know that tho' I *can* stand alone, when it must be, yet I love to lean. M. A. Ripley and Charles Dana passed the 4th of July in Hingham, saw Dora, and say that they found her homesick. The dear girl! would she were here . . . I wonder if she don't laugh now and then, when she thinks of *me* at the head of the consistory group — may it have a better head ere long!

On the evening of the 4th we had a dance in Pilgrim Hall; quite an affair for Brook Farm. The rooms were adorned with superb bouquets, and we had a nice time. . . . A short time ago about twenty of us, at the invitation of Mrs. Russell and her sister Ida, went over to Milton to eat cherries and have a dance. We left here early in the afternoon and came home about twelve that night. They have at Milton a magnificent place, — a commodious, old fashioned house, commanding a fine water prospect, — with a superb garden, — statues, vases, flowers, and everything to delight the eye; — and the table was so *elegantly* filled with cherries, strawberries, etc. — an abundant feast to more than one of the senses. Then too the company was beautiful — among whom were conspicuous the beautiful Geraldine, the intellectual Ida and the lovely Rose. I suppose about fifty visitors were there besides us Brook Farmers. They were invited to meet us and of course all came, for who don't like to look at Brook Farm people? and then too we looked pretty well — we had with us Charles Dana and John [1] and our handsome youths,[2] — Maria Dana,[3] the Macdaniels, Mary Ann Donnelly, etc.

Our friend C. K. N.[4] still interests me. — I permitted him to read what you wrote concerning him. He says he was disappointed that he did not *see* you more that evening — he wished it, but didn't care to be introduced. However he says he heard your voice and was pleased with it. . . . He says you must read the *Seherin* [*von*] *Prevorst* [5] in Margaret Fuller's book. I read it, but it seemed to me to be related in a dull and uninteresting manner.

The other night after tea Rebecca Codman and I spied our friend [6] in a shed back of the wash-room, some of the older boys collected around a barrel of potatoes they were cleaning. He sat with his back to the door reading stories to these boys to their great amusement, so we stood still and listened, to enjoy the fun of teasing him about it afterward. Pretty soon he discovered us and shouted well, and fired potatoes at us, — and after that didn't dare to tell any more stories without now and then sending a potato over his shoulders — Oh! he is a queer one! He regrets Dora's departure much . . .[7] I belong to a group for making fancy

[1] John S. Dwight.

[2] "Our handsome youths" are probably George W. and Burrill Curtis, whom Amelia Russell likened to young Greek gods.

[3] Charles Dana's sister, who later married Osborne Macdaniel.

[4] Charles K. Newcomb.

[5] Frederike Hauffe, a German clairvoyante, daughter of a forester of Prevorst. Margaret Fuller's account of her is in *Summer on the Lakes in 1843*, published in 1844.

[6] "Our friend" is Newcomb.

[7] The next few lines have been quoted in G. W. Cooke's *John Sullivan Dwight*.

articles for sale in Boston. . . . We have been very busy at it of late, and Amelia Russell and I are often much amused at the idea of our having turned milliners and makers of cap-tabs. Our manufacture is quite workmanlike. I assure you, we realize considerable money (!!) from this, and hope, women tho' we be, to have by and by the credit of doing some productive labor. We are now having frequent teachers' meetings to improve our educational practice, and approximate it to our plan. In all this I feel a deep interest, or I would not be thus occupied after nine o'clock at evening. Mother has not been very well for some days, and her eyes are very weak — can scarcely bear the light at all. She will resign for the present her office as chief of the sewing group. Father, John and Fanny are well, — so are all our family by adoption. Do write very soon, and give my love to your mother and sisters when you see them, and don't cease to look forward to Brook Farm.[1] Our Phalanstery cellar is dug. What I have said is only the beginning of what I have to say — Ask Mr. Welles for me, to bring you out here again. Farewell.

Ever with truest love
Mary Ann

Brook Farm, July 7, '44.

Dear Frank,

Whilst I am sitting here with mother, who is resting on the bed, I will write you a somewhat longer note than some you have had. I have been writing to Anna, who has not yet had a line from me since the evening she was here with you, and you have not fared much better. It is too bad I

[1] Anna Parsons's father was opposed to her joining the Brook Farmers and even to her visiting them, except rarely.

know, but could not be helped. Much shall I rejoice when I see the day (which I never expect) that will not find me surrounded by any enslaving circumstances, when I can do just as I would, and live freely. I like our life here better than any I have ever before realized, but the ideal of true life is ever *before* me — we cannot yet attain unto it. Before you get this note you will have seen Carry and heard all her experiences. People here like her very much and John Cheever is quite enthusiastic in his admiration. . . .

Our Phalanstery cellar is dug! John has been elected today as the head of a committee for finding out-of-door work for the boys, an office that has hitherto existed only in the ideal and one of no little magnitude, — especially considering we have such boys as Master James Alfred Kay and Master Jeremiah Cummins Pratt Sloan. However Heaven help him, and Heaven be praised that the good work is going to be undertaken. We have teachers' meetings now at 9 o'clock on Wednesday and Saturday evenings to talk over the education of the children and make some arrangements for having the practice in school accord somewhat with our ideal. . . .

I have joined a group for doing fancy-work to be sold at Mr. Houghton's store in Boston. We have had good success thus far, and make the business profitable, — at least we could if we could get a larger group. I hope herein to find an opportunity of exercising my passional attraction [1] for painting.

Yours with love
Mary Ann

[1] An expression translated from Fourier.

July 16, 1844.

Dear Frank,

. . . This has been a good quieting day, and all nature rejoices in the refreshing rain — never was it more needed. Horace was right, we do have quite "exhilarating" times in walking down to the Hive for our meals in a drenching rain. Tonight mother had a select coffee party in her room, Mrs. Ripley, Mrs. Sloan, etc. Rebecca Codman has been ill for some days, enough so to keep her room, and Fred Cabot has kept himself shut up today, — and now I believe I have about done with the list of invalids. . . .

The Northampton Association have invited Brook Farm people to visit them at a convention on the 20th of this month, and we have voted to send John [1] and Mr. Dana as delegates. I am very glad John is to go, it will be pleasant for him. Next Octobe , delegates from the other Massachusetts associations are to visit us at B. F. I believe Mr. Kay is expected here this week with his little girls. He is going to stay thro' the summer. Since you were here a room, *of the smallest size*, has been manufactured right against ours at the end of the entry, which Maria Dana is going to occupy. I should like it much for a closet. I don't know but we shall have to accommodate some one in our closet next. . . . I wish you could see the flowers upon our table, — a very large and elegant bouquet which Fred brought over from the street.[2] There are a great variety of flowers in it, and some that are entirely new to us. John Codman gathers every wild flower that grows in our vicinity. He is most perfectly at home in the woods, and generally brings with him, when he enters the breakfast room, a hand-

[1] Her brother.

[2] I infer that "the street" is the village of West Roxbury.

some bouquet with which to ornament our Graham table. Charlie Codman (the younger one) is a most beautiful character, — he is very lovely and spiritual, it is delightful to have him for a scholar. Mr. Butterfield is now a member of our association. Sundry improvements in his name have been suggested, and among others, one by Fred Cabot which has now come into pretty general use, viz. Mr. Jonathan B. Fields. Mr. Fitch, the giant, has luckily, been induced to leave us. Mr. Houghton is likewise a member.

Mother wanted me to ask you to look and see what you can find suitable for a thin coat for father, — an every day B. F. coat, — something cheap — will you look? Blueberries are very plenty around here. — The boys frequently go and gather them, and are quite generous with what they bring home. — Delicious raspberries have been gathered from our vines; — however they are sold, and the fact is we don't get many berries now of any kind. How I wish we had currants, — a plenty of them!

I believe Carry left only her watch-key and thimble, — I will send them to Miss Peabody's tomorrow, where you will find them. . . . I hope you will be successful in finding the paste-board.[1] Did you call at Dow's? he was to keep it.

Amelia Russell has been in and kept talking with us till it has become altogether too late for me to write longer. . . . You must excuse the dryness of this letter, for there is a scarcity of materials, and I am shivering with the cold. The stars shine. Tomorrow will be a bright day. . . .

With much love
Mary Ann

[1] Mary Ann Dwight is asking her obliging brother to shop for the materials with which she made up little books of paintings of wild flowers.

Tuesday evening, August 27, '44.

Dear Frank,

I suppose you are wishing to hear from us if only a few lines, — and indeed a few lines is all you would ask, if you knew the multitude of things I have to do, and it is now bed-time. We have just returned from the Eyrie, where we heard Miss Jertz play the "Carnival" and afterwards had a merry time in Mr. Kay's room, where he insisted upon reading Fred's character aloud, in presence of Fred himself, Mr. Ripley, mother and me, — and they made fun enough I can tell you.

But about our own affairs, — matters, I am happy to say, will undoubtedly go right. Indeed, I believe the thing is considered as settled. I am only pained at the false view some others took, and the unfriendliness, which perhaps was not intended, but I feel it to be real.[1] However, I think she feels differently now. Tomorrow I shall write to Anna Parsons, at Mrs. Ripley's request, and invite her to visit us here as soon as she possibly can. Oh! how I shall rejoice to have her here. . . .

Fred's character is perfectly done, one of Anna's best readings. I don't mean it has exhausted the character.

Yours in love
Mary Ann

Brook Farm, Friday p.m., August 30, [*1844*].

Dearest Anna,

I wish you knew how much good your letter did me, and how grateful I am therefor, but you must not insist upon it

[1] Apparently there had been some difficulty about inviting Miss Parsons to stay at Brook Farm. It may have been about this time that the Community found it necessary to charge a small fee for visitors.

that I don't love you, — yes, you, Anna Parsons, and not alone that ideal you talk so much about. I think of thee . . . with all thy feebleness and thy faults, — with all thy ultraisms, and even thy old mania for meetings, — I forget that thou art an "inseer" and I love thee none the less. Why, thou art ungrateful not to acknowledge that I love thee, and now I would have thee to know that I cannot think of living any longer without thee. There is a void that you must come and fill, and you must stay with us at least a week. . . . We have some fine spirits here with whom you must become acquainted, and for your sake and for theirs, I would have you meet. I don't know when you would most enjoy coming, our population is so changing. Should think you would like best to be here when Mr. Parker[1] preaches his first sermons and makes his first visit, and I believe he is expected home next week. — Amelia Russell is now absent, but will be here, I suppose, next Wednesday. I shall want her here. Fanny Macdaniel has gone to New York, and will probably stay a fortnight or longer, but perhaps not so long. She is quite desirous of becoming acquainted with you. Now Anna, come you must. All that myself and others can do for you to make you happy here, shall be done. If you only knew how much good you would do — and then you will learn somewhat of our life.

[1] Theodore Parker, after a period of painful excitement and disillusion caused by theological differences between himself and his Unitarian brethren, had had a nervous breakdown and gone abroad to rest. According to one of his biographers, John White Chadwick, he "rested like fury"; nevertheless he returned Sept. 1, 1844 in good spirits to his West Roxbury Church, which had heartily supported him during the controversy over his "heresy." When called to Boston in 1846, he was succeeded for a few months in West Roxbury by Channing.

Thank you for your ready compliance with my requests. I am confident that you read Fred truly, — I think I know him well and you have entirely satisfied me. It is a very lifelike picture that you have drawn of him; you have given all that Mr. Orvis gave, and a great deal more. You have, to say the least, taken my point of view, and seen him as I see him. He was perfectly willing that you should have read his letter, and I thought I had expressed this to you when I wrote. Mr. Orvis's notes you shall have as soon as Fred or I find time to copy them and your notes of Fred shall be returned to you soon. . . . Fred's mother didn't recognize him from your notes, — it must be that she don't see just the same person in him that we do. Mrs. Ward says she don't know him well enough to judge at all, — thinks much very good. Mr. Ripley and Mr. Kay think it excellent. Fred has had thoughts of writing to you to learn more about those *chained devils* (but I don't believe he'll get time). I have frequently heard him allude to the said devils, or to one in particular, when I have been talking with him, and he would seem deeply grieved and desponding; he would like to ask you of their nature and what he shall do to exorcise them. Friend Newcomb has gone to Katskill, so I could not give him your message. He will be back here next Wednesday, I believe. I forgot to say that Fred feels well satisfied with your reading of him.

We have had some pleasant guests since I last wrote. A visit from William H. Channing,[1] — need I tell you how

[1] William Henry Channing, nephew of the great champion of Unitarianism, began his own career as a Unitarian minister. About this date he was preaching, whenever and wherever he could, Christian socialism, antislavery, and the upbuilding of the spiritual life. He had eloquence and personal magnetism and a "benign and beautiful presence."

much I enjoyed it? Mr. Alcott[1] has been here too; and today is a sad day with us for we have parted with Mr. Kay and his little girls; with Miss Sophy Jertz, — an intimate friend of Fanny Macdaniel's, a Norwegian lady, one of the sweetest and most harmonious persons I ever met. She has light hair, and earnest mild blue eyes — is well versed in Fourier, — that is to say, she is a *phalansterian;* and better than all, she is inspired with music, it pervades her whole manner, and her voice is music itself, and she performs on the piano-forte, second only to Frederick Rakemann. Then we have had two Frenchmen who came in her train, likewise phalansterians, Mons. Bernard, and Mons. Quailke, both men of much depth of mind. Mons. B. could hardly speak a word of English; Mons. Bernard left today with Miss Jertz but will return again on Sunday to stay a little while longer.

And now I must interest you in our fancy group, for which and from which I hope great things, — nothing less than the elevation of woman to independence, and an acknowledged equality with man. Many thoughts on this subject have been struggling in my mind ever since I came to Brook Farm, and now, I think I see how it will all be accomplished. Women must become producers of marketable articles; women must make money and earn their support independently of man. So we, with a little borrowed capital (say twenty-five or thirty dollars; by we, I mean a large part of the women here), have purchased materials, and made up in one week about forty-five dollars worth of elegant and tasteful caps, capes, collars, undersleeves, etc., etc., — which we sent in to Hutchinson and Holmes, who

[1] Amos Bronson Alcott made occasional visits and gave "talks" at the Farm.

have agreed to take all we can make. If they find a ready sale, we shall be greatly encouraged, — and be able to go on extending our business, as far as our time and numbers will allow. Of course, if we succeed (and we are determined we will), it will be very desirable for other ladies to come here on purpose to take a part in our fancy work; then our domestic work which now presses too heavily, will get more divided, and we shall each have less house-work and more fancy work. By and by, when funds accumulate (!) we may start other branches of business, so that all our proceeds must be applied to the elevation of woman forever. Take a spiritual view of the matter. Raise woman to be the equal of man, and what intellectual developments may we not expect? How the whole aspect of society will be changed! And this is the great work, is it not, that Association in its present early stage has to do? Do, as you love and honor your sex, bear our fancy group in mind, and bring or send us patterns and designs of every sort of thing you see or can conceive of that will be useful to us. We want your mother here. We want your sister Elizabeth; she will come I hope, by and by. For one week I have indulged my passional attraction and painted to my heart's content. Mr. Kay is the patron of our group. I esteem and love him more, the more I know him. Tell Dora, had she been here during his last visit, she could not help loving him. It is my devotion to fancy work and to education that have not left me a minute to spare for writing, reading or thinking on aught else. We are about organizing children into groups for labor and education, a very important step and by no means an easy one. Mr. Orvis is to be the director for the boys and as they look to me for the girls, it must occupy considerable of my time.

You can't think how deeply I feel my *incompetency* for this work. . . .

Write immediately and tell me that you will come, and if you can, tell me when. Recollect Parker will be here probably in a week from tomorrow. Perhaps Hannah Ripley, Dora, etc. will make us the long talked of visit and bring you with them — in which case they will *not* take you home with them. Much love to all.

Mary-Ann

[1844?]

My dear Anna,

This is good news indeed that you are coming. And it is true that you have no time to lose, so come as soon as you can. I shall look for you by the middle of the week. — I suppose there is no doubt but that you can have a room at the Eyrie. I think Mr. R. told you that if you and Fanny came the price would be $2 for you, $4 with Fanny. If you come alone, he thinks it will be something more for you, perhaps $3, but Mr. Dana must (with the financial council) determine it, and he is not here today. I am so glad you are coming! so are others. I have hardly a doubt but Fanny will come. . . .

Ever with love
Marianne

Brook Farm, Sept. 3, 1844.

Dearest Anna,

Thou art safe,[1] and most fervently do I thank Heaven, I long to see thee and fold my arms around thee, that I may realize that thou hast really escaped after being in such imminent danger. I have been with thee in the deep ever

[1] Anna Parsons's visit did not take place as planned, but was prevented by an accident, the nature of which must be inferred from this letter.

since reading thy thrilling letter, — the awful scene is present to me continually. — Yet so unreal, — so like a fearful dream, that I can hardly conceive it can have actually occurred.

Oh! it must have been frightful — it must have been full of horrors, — the *thought* of it is so to me now, and I turn for relief to the sweet calmness, the holy resignation which sustained *your* soul at that trying moment. Beautiful indeed is it to die as you would have died, — the spirit disturbed with no thought of self, — yet may the angels in bliss forgive my joy, that instead of floating gently into heaven, you floated back to earth. You must all have had much physical, as well as mental suffering, — poor Mrs. Peabody! It must have been trying indeed to see her, and how much she must have suffered. I long to hear from you all again. — I cannot but hope that *you* will recover from the sad effects of the accident much sooner than you anticipate. It seems to me that the spirit which has borne you up, will conquer, and as your mind recovers from the shock, strength and health will be restored to your frame.

Thursday, half past five, a.m.

I found my head and eyes so weak evening before last (but don't imagine this is common) that I was obliged to stop writing, and all day yesterday I was visited with a severe headache. I am afraid to attempt to write much at this early hour but will try to have a package ready for Mrs. Ripley to take to Boston for you. I send Mr. Orvis's notes of Fred, and didn't think to ask him whether he wants them back or not. So keep them until I send you word, for I *guess* he has another copy. He returns your notes.[1]

[1] *I.e.* notes on Fred Cabot's character from a reading by Miss Parsons.

Oh! how truly you have read him. Mrs. Follen says it is perfect; that, knowing him thoroughly as she does, she could not have written it half so well. . . .

I wish I could hear from you today, and from the other drowned ones. Why, Anna dear, tell Helen I think you have realized what she said of you, that if "you were to be drowned, you'd save yourself." Thus has it happened unto you, you dear child. Somehow the idea that a light, frail thing like you, with more of the *aromal* than the material in your nature, could ever drown — Yet I shudder when I think how near it came to being a fact. I think you owe your safety, in great part, to your composure, which enabled you to breathe and thus to float. . . . I must tell you that I am becoming superstitious. That same Friday p.m. my spirit was so vexed and troubled and uneasy, that I have often thought of it since with pain, and wondered at the cause. I was most uncomfortable, and *unaccountably* so, both physically and spiritually, — it seemed to me something was going wrong, — that I was not where I would be and ought to be. What did it mean? Had my spirit some unconscious feeling that a loved one was at the mercy of the waves, — that danger was near; — that some dreadful blow threatened me? May-be so.

Tell Dora the nursery is increasing, — in one fortnight three babies were born unto Brook Farm Association. The little stranger, Charles Fourier Colson,[1] made his appearance last Sunday — little Miss Hastings [2] a few days previous, and little Miss Patterson first of all. They are all *fine* babies — *beautiful* babies, etc., etc. — so smart that they

[1] Son of Colson, the shoemaker.

[2] Buckley Hastings, her father, was in the expressing, shipping, and purveying department of the Farm.

go a-visiting, and will no doubt soon be able to utter their first words, — which of course we expect will be "groups and series" and "association." They are the most peaceable little bodies and have given nobody any trouble by their appearance among us! Oh, the blessedness of Association! I've no doubt Dora will rejoice with us that these interesting adventures are over so quietly and happily.

Parker has not yet been to Brook Farm. Next Sunday we shall go to hear him preach. Wish you could get well enough to come, then I would keep you. Come you must, as soon as possible — I won't have a refusal, so make up your mind to it. Frank mentioned it to your father, and found him inclined to favor your coming — so you have no excuse under heaven.

Do write very soon, and give my love, any quantity of it, to all. I am impatient to hear.

With much love
Mary Ann

Thursday a.m., Sept. 5, 1844.

Dear Frank,

Anna's letter was thrilling, and was a great shock to me, — I felt as if I had been with them in the waves. But, thank Heaven! they were saved, almost by miracle. . . . I'm sorry not to have her visit *now*, but trust she will come.

The third little stranger, Charles Fourier Colson, was born to B. F. A.[1] last Sunday, — just a fortnight after the arrival of the first one. . . .

Be sure to come out Saturday, that you hear Mr. Parker. The Ripleys, John and Fred have been to see him and find him looking well, and appearing just the same. Mrs. R.

[1] Brook Farm Association.

says as soon as he and Mr. Ripley met, they fell to making poems.

Oh! how the men, and women too, do talk "*groups and series*" here. It is as bad as politics.

Am afraid to write more, because my head aches, so adieu.

Mary Ann

Oh! tell everybody that B. F. fancy articles are to be had at Holmes' and Hutchinson's, near King's — and at Mr. Houghton's. We want to advertize by sending our friends there. Mr. Orvis has promised to read Mary's [1] character as soon as he can.

Brook Farm, Wed. p.m., Sept. 18, '44.

Dearest Anna,

I had become very impatient to hear from you, when Monday evening came your very welcome letter. I rejoice that all of you drowned ones are so far convalescent, and that there is a prospect that I shall see your sweet face and Dora's very soon. . . . Hannah Ripley and Dora have been long expected, and we are all glad that you are coming with them and hope Mrs. Wilder and Cordelia are better and well enough for Dora to leave. Mary Lincoln will probably come out on Saturday with Harriet Jackson to pass a few days, — they were out here an hour or so last week — came on horseback. Mr. Brownson [2] is expected to be here next Sunday, in which I don't rejoice, but many are glad; — whether this will be an inducement to you

[1] Probably Mary Bullard.

[2] Orestes Augustus Brownson had been of assistance to Brook Farm through his favorable article in the Democratic Review in 1842. He had become a Roman Catholic in the spring of 1844. He was a man who frequently aroused opposition by his bad manners in carrying on discussions.

Hingham people to come, I can't tell, but throw it out at a venture. — It needn't prevent you at any rate, for it will spoil none of our pleasure. — You shall do as you please, dear Anna, about the time for that promised week's visit; only bear in mind that we are depending on it. . . . Let it be in October, if you possibly can — I want you whilst the weather is comfortably warm — when the autumn foliage is in its richest, gladdest hues, — when we can walk in the woods by moonlight. . . . Now, Anna, — Don't make it too late in the season, for I'm such a *cold* creature that I shan't enjoy walking with you in dreary November.

I wonder if you have perceived anything unusual yet in the style of my letter, or any change in the handwriting sufficient to indicate that the feeling of maternity has taken full possession of me. If you have not, then must I tell you that I have two boys, one eight, the other eleven years old confided to my care. Their father is a widower, their names, Caspar and William Henry Goldermann. I assure you it is no light thing to be thus suddenly and unexpectedly seized with the maternal sentiment; those people who have come by it in the natural way can have no idea of my feelings. I have fixed "my boys" as everyone here calls them, very comfortably into Dora's room — and let her imagine with what changed feelings I now enter that little room, which she endeared to me, and which her memory still hallows. The boys have been here but a day and a half — I tremble to think of the task I have undertaken, and I have to stand all manner and degrees of joking.

There is some excitement here just now (tell Dora) about the people who want to be married and have "spoken for rooms" large enough for two, and are mad and vexed, because in our present crowded state, they can't have them. . . .[1]

You ask my impression of Mr. Parker. I heard him on the first Sunday, — have not yet had any conversation with him. He preached well, — yes, well, even for him, — his manner perhaps more simple and natural than before. He gave the most excellent statistics for associationists — said everything leading directly to Association, — but not a word for it, — stopped short of the mark, which he *must* reach, if he is true. I don't want to see him in a false position, and I feel that he is.

I have not time to say more, but must tell you, that I shall try to get up a party to go into Boston to the New England Fourier meeting, next Friday evening — and that we have just formed a Fourier class for Monday and Thursday evenings out here, — a class to study Fourier's works, conducted by Mr. Ripley, — and that countless other classes, enough to make one's brain whirl, are about forming.

Excuse my haste, as it is nearer six than I thought. . . .

Tell Dora, J. Cheever will be here next Sunday. He will not tell *where* he is going.

Ever thine
Mary Ann

Thurs. a.m., Sept. 19, '44.

Dear Frank,

. . . Yesterday Mr. List and Mr. Reynolds were unanimously expelled from the carpenter's group in consequence of their being discordant elements, — so they

[1] Lindsay Swift in his *Brook Farm*, p. 117, remarks that "Fourteen marriages have been traced to friendships begun at Brook Farm and the record of unhappy unions is small."

MARIANNE DWIGHT

Who wrote the letters.

went to the general direction requesting to be furnished with work, and that body have set them to work upon the frame of the Phalanstery, — so they are working right in the midst of the group, but not of the group, doing just what they are told to do, — a sort of solitary labor and imprisonment. It is quite an amusing state of things. The group who thought to get rid of their company are foiled in that.

It is a most magnificent day — the perfection of autumn, except that we have needed rain for a long time — And what are you about? The same old round of labor I suppose, only you may be anxiously laying new plans. Oh! that we could prepare ourselves to meet all changes and disappointments without any vexation of spirit, and with a cheerful trust that all will work out right. — Nay, better, if we could feel that all is right now! But there is a sense in which all is not right, and perhaps it is this that disturbs us. I wish you were here, Frank, tho' I don't feel inclined to hurry you. For myself, I would not exchange this life for any I have ever led. I could not feel contented again with the life of isolated houses, and the conventions of civilization. I enjoy here more than I ever enjoyed — and it is true likewise that I have had some very keen suffering — In the present state of Association and with my sensibilities I feel that I must be continually exposed to suffering; — but constant activity is a good counterpoise, — and life is so full and rich here, that I feel as if my experience were valuable, and I were *growing* somewhat faster than when I lived in Boston. We have thought much of your circumstances and long to have you settled here with us, and shall rejoice when you are *ready* to come, — but I repeat we would not hurry you. . . .

Our Fourier class went off finely — some people from the street came over. Hope to go to Boston tomorrow evening, but don't know. If we do, shall stop at E. P. Peabody's I suppose.

Hearing a great hurrah, I have just been to the window, and lo! Martin and a group of boys returning from their work, — little Fourierites, with banners flying. I believe if they have been idle, the banners are not permitted to wave. The boys are really getting to enjoy their work, and these banners are a grand excitement. Probably the fancy group will have to work them a very handsome one. . . .

Yours ever affectionately
Mary Ann

Wed. evening, Oct. [*9th*], *1844.*

Dear Frank,

Your letter came safely, — I believe I've nothing new to tell you, — except that my air-tight stove is up and promises to administer much to our comfort. I feel quite tired tonight with my cold and the work together, — hardly fit to handle a pen, — but nevertheless have finished a letter to Anna, begging her to tell me when she'll come. . . . I send it to you by Fred and hope you will see him. The long letter you sent was well worth the sending, and well worth our reading, but it breathes a sadder tone than I could wish, and I hope you will be enabled to look more on the sunny side of things and to look always with the eye of faith. M. A. Williams is very low. I should not be surprised at her death any time. . . .

With much love
Mary Ann

Thursday p.m., Oct. [*10th*], *1844*.

Dear Frank,

We have had some little excitement since dinner. I had gone about half-way home, when I met Rebecca flying with all speed towards the Hive. Said she, "I fear the Pilgrim House is on fire." I raced home, flew into my room — found smoke pouring out around my stove and fire place, — opened my closet and expected to see the flames burst out there very quickly. I thought what I must first save, — unlocked a drawer and put $13 or $14 into my pocket. Took down all the clothes from the closet, and ran with them to the rock behind the house — came back to seize something else and met Mr. Channing at my door, who said there was no need of it, for they would soon conquer the fire. He took away my stove, they filled up my room with buckets of water, and prepared to tear down the plastering if necessary. Meantime there was a greater fracas in the ironing room under mine, where stood the stove and where through a crack, the wood work around the chimney was seen to be in flames. Mr. Jenkins took an axe, knocked away the plaster, — discovered a flame 10 inches broad which must (had there been a short delay) have fired the house, but water was thrown on and it was stopped. People have been mightily amused at the idea of my saving my ward-robe down behind the rock!! I have not yet learned why the fire caught — perhaps some of Mr. Codman's bungling in putting up the stove.

Last evening we had a meeting of the Association — *Friday a.m.* You see I have been interrupted, dear Frank — I now steal time to finish, for I must put my room in order after the confusion of the fire. About the meeting.

Our John [1] opened it with some dismal and discouraging remarks about the state of feeling here. I don't know what has got into him, but he was very unlike himself. J. O.[1] spoke very cheeringly, truthfully and encouragingly, and the result was hopeful and good. We passed a vote that the financial council should pay to any needy person who applies $3.00 of his stipend, and so on thro' the whole, and that no more shall be paid to any one until each has his three dollars. — Mr. Channing said to me the next day, "Was you not very much delighted with our friend, John Orvis, last night?" I said I was glad that he said what he did. "Yes, indeed," said he, "it was fine, — he was the *salvation* of the meeting."

By the way, John O. is sick in his room — has a very severe cold upon his lungs. Many of us have had colds. Mrs. Palisse,[2] Eunice, Maria, Eaton,[2] and Amelia has her throat done up and looks like a mummy.

Thank you for the drawing paper, which I like much. I am late about my work, or I would write more. How is Anna? She was right to come back that morning. My love to her. Tell her about the fire.

With much love
Marianne

Brook Farm, Tuesday eve., Oct. 29, 1844.

Dearest Anna,

. . . It is tea-time. I sit alone in my snug little room. Fred, our "good Fred" [3] has been spending a half hour in

[1] When Miss Dwight speaks of "John," she invariably means her brother, John S. Dwight. "J. O." is John Orvis.

[2] Mrs. Palisse, wife of Jean M. Palisse, the Swiss engineer; Eaton, sometimes called "Old Solidarity."

[3] The reader will already have noticed that Miss Dwight has a marked partiality for Fred Cabot's society.

relieving me of the head-ache, which has been tormenting me all day, and has positively forbidden me to go down to tea, and engaged to find some one to supply my place in washing cups, etc., after tea. It will not be mother, for she is having a coffee party at the Eyrie, and as our friend Mr. N. is a lover of coffee, undoubtedly he will be a partaker. We have had, what you so much desired, a regular, earnest storm, — a hard rain and plenty of wind. Had quite an exhilarating walk down to breakfast, with Fanny — went from house to house in the consistory; — was asked by C. N.[1] if I had written to you yet, — when I reached the Pilgrim House found Mrs. Hosmer and Fred exchanging rooms; — spent a little time looking on, and assisting John Orvis in putting to rights, for you know he is to room with Fred. Dinner time came ere long — it rained in torrents; — our covered wagon or omnibus drove up to the door to take such passengers as wished to ride down to the Hive, so nine or ten of us packed ourselves into it, and were brought safely home again after dinner. My afternoon has been spent at the Cottage, — so much of the events of the day. For this evening, we are anticipating a dance in Pilgrim Hall in honor of Popleston's departure. The boys have gone to Dedham for a fiddler — I wish *you* were here, I should like so much to have you see one of our dances. I wish, if I feel able, to go down for a short time, as a looker on.

I passed yesterday p.m. in Miss Russell's room, at fancy work — from which I rested about three quarters of an hour, and read to her from Cranch's poems.

I should like to have you peep into my neighbours' room and see the arrangements. The sublime J. O. has a high

[1] Charles K. Newcomb.

bedstead which stands directly *over* that of Fred, — who being *small* and young is thus accommodated with a sort of trundle bed to be drawn out at night! Oh! what ingenious beings they are!

When I returned to my desolate room on Sunday, after taking leave of you and Dora, you can hardly imagine how I felt, — I knew that I should miss you so much. Fred came in, and brought his grasses, which I fell to helping him arrange. He seemed to be rather blue, and soon his brother Frank joined us. We had a pretty good talk, — some puns and jokes,[1] — among others, Frank brought forward this, which is so good I can remember it. "Where was the first fighting? Ans. In chaos, where *Nihil fit.*" I suppose you know Latin enough to understand that, don't you? If you don't, ask some more learned friend to explain. Fred was restored to happiness during the tea hour, by beating his brother at chess.

You see how little material I have to make out a letter with, as I am reduced to the necessity of telling you the merest commonplaces. But then I know that you, who have been here, can look behind these little facts, and see more than they tell to everyone.

The fiddler must have arrived, for I hear the scraping of the fiddle! . . .

I can't very well write more now on account of my head, — perhaps may add a line ere bed-time.

Half past eleven.

The dance is over. — I have been a spectator for two hours. It was a beautiful dance. I was standing near

[1] This love of puns, mostly bad, as they seem to us, was not confined to Brook Farmers. It is noticeable in the diaries of seventeenth century Puritans and throughout the lighter poems and the prose of Oliver Wendell Holmes.

Charlie N., speaking with Amelia, when he went across the room, brought a seat and placed it beside him for me. From *him* I felt the kindness, and we all three sat there together the whole evening. — I wish you could have seen his heavenly smile when I left the room and he bade me good-night. Of course we sat together almost in silence.

And now good night, — I must have sleep and rest. — May you be enjoying the same, and may the spirits of loved ones visit you in your dreams. . . .

Your
Mary Ann

Brook Farm, Nov. 1, '44.

Dear Frank,

. . . Tuesday evening we had a dance for Popleston's farewell, and Pop has really gone. — I can hardly feel that it is so. — He was so amiable, and such an ornament here, that I hated to have him go. Thursday was appointed for the quarterly Association convention, and delegates were invited from Northampton and Hopedale. The Northamptons didn't come. Six male Hopedales arrived and several women, and we managed to find them each a place to sleep. In the evening we had quite an interesting meeting, tho' nothing remarkable. Mr. Ballou spoke a good deal. But for this meeting we should have had a Shakespeare reading; now I suppose it will come off next Thursday. . . .

Mr. Orvis and Frederick have moved into the next room to mine, — another move in our entry is yet to be made. Oh! when will our habitations be fixed? If it be true, as a favorite writer says, that three removals, for loss, are equivalent to one fire, — then surely B. F. cannot long have much left to lose. The move to which I refer is this, — Caspar and Willie [1] are coming into the little room or closet that Anna lately occupied. They don't like the idea much because they can't have any parties (!) in so small a room. I suppose when the Phalanstery is done the expansion will be in proportion to the present cramming or condensation. . . .

Your affectionate
Mary Ann

Thursday a.m., Nov. 14, '44.

Dear brother,

. . . Fanny received your note this morning by John. She has decided not to go in next Saturday unless there should be some way provided here for her to return at night, which is not in the least probable. . . . Will it not comfort you to know that Amelia [2] (who sends her *love* to you) will be in Boston from Friday till Monday? — and here will be a fine opportunity for you to display your gallantry, and pay your devoirs in a manner which I doubt not will be very acceptable to her. You can ask her to go to the concert with you in Fanny's place, in case Fanny should not go in! Won't this be rather agreeable than otherwise? Amelia says you must call and see her at No. 2 Franklin Place (I believe, she *may* have said F. Street). . . .

We have had some very dark nights, and begin to meet with various adventures in our evening walks, — and to hear frightful stories of last winter's adventures. — I think I shall have to own a lantern. I've borrowed one, and in

[1] The Goldermann children, her new charges.

[2] Mary Ann Dwight's references to Amelia Russell in letters to her brother Frank have a slight flavor of match-making.

going down to the Hive the other night, I heard a heavy fall down, down, down the hill at my left, which startled me, and frightened me somewhat, — I turned and listened, — no sound, — I spoke, — and soon a step, and the not-to-be-mistaken voice of — *List*, who called me by name. He had slipped and slid down the hill. He came uninjured however, took my lantern, offered his arm, and we went in a very friendly way to the Hive. The same evening, Newcomb got lost in the dark, and ran against a cart. . . .

Adieu.

Come Sunday.

Mary Ann

Wed. evening, Dec. 4, '44.

Dear Frank,

It is late, and my room grows cold, but I will write a word and trust to Providence for a chance to send to you and Anna tomorrow. I should like to have the varnish pretty soon, (no matter if you don't bring it till Saturday, if you can come then), and if you could find at Cotton's or some other place some pretty colored paper for lining and get me a yard of good thick narrow ribbon (the *three cent width*) of about the same color, it would oblige me much, and I will pay for them. Will you call at Ashton's and other places and look at the paper lamp shades, the painted ones, so as to tell me if they are (as Mary Osgood thought) painted on common paper, and in the common way?

Amelia commenced a new class this evening, has been teaching grown gentlemen to dance, twelve of them — just imagine it. She sends her love to you. . . . M. A. Williams is *very low* — Little Anna Foord is ill, and C. Newcomb and Fred are on the sick list today, tho' not very bad.

Elmira too, is quite sick. I'm glad you didn't come out Sunday, for the walking was horrid.

Write and tell us how you are.

In haste
Affectionately
Mary Ann

The Goldermanns have gone not to return. Don't you congratulate me on my release?

Brook Farm, Dec. 14, '44.

Dearest Anna

. . . I think Fanny will go in to the concert this evening and I hope you will see her, and *perhaps* you will have a note ready for me, and the notes for Mr. N. I am sorry to make so poor a return for your excellent letter, — even now I have not a quiet hour, but am superintending a painting lesson, and of course cannot write steadily. I thought I would not go in to the concert tonight because I am very busy, and wish, when I go, to have a few hours to spend in Boston. Thank you for all the interesting things you said in your note. Mr. N. would like to have you write your impressions for him; — I don't imagine that he is any hurry for his MS but only impatient to learn your impressions,[1] and therefore he said, ask her to read it *soon* — I know he would be disappointed to have it sent back unread. He was struck with what you said in your note, — said jestingly he "didn't believe but you was a *cheat*, and had read it with your eyes."[2] . . .

[1] Anna Parsons is evidently adding to her former reading of Newcomb's character.

[2] Instead of by the sense of touch. But, as Miss Orvis explains, Anna Parsons was well known to be incapable of any form of cheating.

Have I ever told you about our retrenchment, dearest Anna? . . . You know it is one of our rules not to incur any debt, but to pay as we go along — well, we found that we could not be sure of commanding ready money this winter sufficient to pay our expenses, so we agreed to retrench in our table fare, in order to make a saving and come within the means we can command. It was really cheering to see how readily this measure was adopted. We now set one of the long tables in our old style for boarders, scholars and visitors, — and a *few associates* who feel that their *health* requires (!) the use of meat, tea, etc. At the other tables we have no meat, no tea, nor butter, nor sugar. This "retrenchment" has afforded us no little amusement. We are not at a loss for something to eat, — have good potatoes, turnips, squashes, etc., etc., and puddings. At our breakfast table I counted nine different articles this morning; so we can't complain of want of variety. Our New York friends are pitying us very much and wonder what we can have left to eat. For my own part, I think much good will come out of it. I trust our people will find by and by that meat and tea have lost their relish, and that there is something better. Perhaps we shall have fewer head-aches, etc. Charlie N. sat at the *no* retrenchment table at *one* meal, but has come home to us again, and is excepted from the general rule and allowed to have tea and butter brought to him.[1] Our breakfast these short days is ready precisely at seven and, in order to make people punctual, Mr. Capen carries the dishes off at exactly half-past. Here again, friend N. is excepted, as he ought to be. We hear that many small associations are

[1] Miss Dwight, like all others who knew Newcomb, does not question the justice of treating him as an exceptional being.

stopped, or will stop soon. — Some good will come of this. *We* only have to *retrench.* Friends of Association in New York and elsewhere are beginning to see the need of concentrating their efforts in some one undertaking, and it is to Brook Farm that they look. Mr. Kay regards our condition as much more prosperous and hopeful than when he was here in the summer. No matter if we are to have a hard winter in some respects, we know how to make sunshine around us and to wear smiling faces. What a hindrance to us is our climate!

I *do* love the country, even in winter. The morning after this snow storm, I went down to the Hive through drifts higher than my head, stepped on a stone wall to get through one. Oh! the snow has been so beautiful and the air and the sky so clear and fine, and everything so much brighter, and more cheerful than winter in Boston. . . .

We had two comedies performed Thursday evening and to admiration. The "dramatic corps" have built a regular stage, and are to have scenery for *Pizarro*[1] three weeks hence. I don't quite approve of their theatricals now, because I think they occupy more time than, in our present state, we can afford to give. I wish you would invite your friend Seth Welles to ride out here with you very soon. I wish you would write me something about the trees and flowers. How do pines affect you? How certain flowers? Love to each and all. Hope to see you soon.

Lovingly
Mary Ann

[1] By Sheridan.

Brook Farm, Dec. 22, 1844.

Dearest Anna,[1]

Oh for time to write and tell you all I have heard today from Brisbane [2] and all the other things that interest me. . . . He arrived last evening. This morning we assembled at half past ten to hear what he had to say. He promised us for the forenoon merely the history of his travels in Europe, but it was mingled with so much philosophy — his views were so broad and deep, his language so eloquent and forcible, that we could not but feel gratified and instructed. What he said of nationalities was very fine, — that in each nation we see a predominating sentiment, which characterizes it throughout. In England familism is predominant.[3] This marks the English landscape, dotting it with cottage and manor houses. This pervades the industry of the nation, in which the useful always predominates — they manufacture useful articles, well made, of good material, etc. In France, *cabalism* is the ruling sentiment, — social feeling, love of variety, of amusements, etc., mark the people. Hence people of fortune forsake the country and flock into the cities. In all their manufactures they have the elegant in view, — usefulness, durability are not so much regarded as outside show and elegance. He gave us a most beautiful and vivid picture of Paris, with its broad streets, its palaces, foun-

[1] This letter is quoted in G. W. Cooke's *John Sullivan Dwight*.

[2] Albert Brisbane, born 1809 at Batavia, New York, a traveled man of independent means, devoted his life to the spread in America of Fourier's plan for social reform. His most distinguished and influential converts were Horace Greeley of the Tribune and George Ripley of Brook Farm.

[3] The ability to generalize in this impressive but superficial fashion was Brisbane's best asset as a speaker. Educated Americans were eager for a philosophy which should explain to them their own society. Compare Emerson's essay (really a lecture), *Civilization*.

tains, statues, etc. — He actually carried us there with him and showed us all this magnificence and let us see for ourselves what, even in civilization, the combined efforts of men can do. He said he never witnessed so much life and activity, — never felt so truly the greatness of man. He says England has been raised up for this purpose, to serve as the great industrial school of the world. The aristocracy have disciplined the mass of the people, have made them learn to work and kept them working, — hence has resulted a race of men inured to toil, capable of subduing nature, never recoiling from the material — from such a people alone, could have come the great steamboats, the railroads, etc. The destiny of France has been to break down the feudal spirit of the middle ages, to destroy catholicism and aristocracy. He gave a fine picture of the history of France up to her present speculative time, asserted that only in that country, amidst such a people, could such a genius as Fourier have been born. Both nations have done their part towards bringing about the state of harmony to which we look forward.

He spoke in conclusion of man's right to the soil and to education. In England the land was centuries ago seized upon by the right of the sword and held by individuals as their property and left to their heirs, and so held that it cannot go out of the families. The whole soil of England is owned by about a hundred families. Twelve or fifteen millions of her people have no other way of subsistence than to cul—

Sunday evening.

I was suddenly interrupted here to listen again to Brisbane, — 'tis now time I was in bed. To resume — than to cultivate the soil, so they are wholly in the power of the first landed proprietors; they must starve or cultivate it on the owner's terms! What a state of things!

Mr. Brisbane spoke finely of Eugène Sue, who is a thorough associationist and understands well the science. His next novel is to be devoted *wholly* to *Association.* His novels are read by a million of people. Think what a propagator of our doctrines we have in him. This p.m., Mr. B. spoke on the prospects of Association in France, — which he considers rather miserable and hopeless. *Here* is the field, — and here at Brook Farm must the efforts of all be concentrated. Probably Mr. B. will come and live with us. But I have no time to tell you anything that was planned and devised for this next year's operations. It is hopeful, is it not? that we have this *first* year, a dividend of profits amounting to 1445 dollars.

Mr. Newcomb has gone to pass Christmas in Providence. Our sister associate M. A. Williams was, this morning, released from her severe sufferings by death. — The first death that has occurred here — A beautiful grove of cypress trees back of our house has been selected for her grave. She has been taken care of in the best and kindest manner, and received the universal sympathy; nowhere else could this poor woman, who has no near relatives and no property, have fared so well. Here is one of the pleasantest blessings of Association. . . .

In haste and in love, Yours

Mary Ann

Brook Farm, Monday, Dec. 30, 1844.

Dearest Anna,

I feel as if I hadn't really a minute for myself or my friends, such entire devotion does this great work of Association demand; but I give my pleasantest and happiest thoughts often to those I love, when my hands are at work in this vast machinery. For the last few days my spirit has not been here, but with those who are dear to me in Boston. How I have longed to be with you and how real and childish was my disappointment to be "conquested" thus by weather — and prevented from fulfilling my intention of going in Friday or Saturday. I lost my only opportunity of sending over to the street Saturday morning for the omnibus, and had nothing to do, but submit with what grace I could and lose seeing the dear ones at your house, and Frank and the concert, etc. The snow is very deep here. Ten times on Saturday I put on india rubbers, cloak, etc., for my various walks to and fro, and did not go to dinner either, and you have no idea how completely tired out the evening found me. It is no little exercise to walk thro' such snow. I scolded well about the lazy men, for not having shovelled paths. I told them I never dreamed of a place where the men paid so little attention to the comfort of the women. This was at the tea-table. The result was the formation of a shovelling group, which will probably soon take scientific form. Yesterday I was unable to go out until evening when I felt that I must go to our business meeting at the Hive. John Orvis too has wanted much to go to Boston, and he wants to see you, so we had much sympathy together. Fred has been disappointed likewise, has been sick all the week, — fortunately for himself, was at home with his mother. I wonder if it will put any thing more than the truth into that wondrous wise head of yours if I tell you that it has been lonely enough here during his absence. Yesterday his brother Frank brought him over here to see us, and today the perverse youth will go to Boston. Mary has written him out a note and I suppose all the powers can't keep him at home any longer, — but he is not well enough to go. I must tell you of almost the only good time I've had for a week or two. Frank Cabot came over Christmas p.m. We made him stay to our evening party. It was glorious moonlight, and an unrivalled evening and John Orvis and I took it into our heads to accompany him part way home. Oh, if you had been with us! We had a fine talk.

You ask how many flirtations I carry on now. Why, you saucy thing, I will box your ears when I see you. But I never "*evade.*" *One* with almost any body — no, one with Christopher List, — two with J. Orvis, and Miss Russell says, "and *seven with Fred.*" Now the fact is I *never flirt*, — the word is out of my dictionary. Tell Celia, Charles Dana has just come in and is sitting here very sociably in my room as I write. He is a beautiful being. Mr. List has left us for a while. — What a strange being! — I should like to have you read him for me. . . .

I took a time when I was fit for nothing else and have dressed out my glass and bureau much to my liking. Between you and me I have little opinion that Mrs. ——'s is a proper place for our fancy work. To-day I am going to send in some pretty card-cases I've been painting on wood to Miss Wall's and a few other things. This business will never be arranged to our satisfaction until we've a store of our own. . . .

Fanny and Eunice Macdaniel have become members of the Association, particularly Fanny. We have also the Palisse family, who are just the right sort. When shall we have A. Q. T. P.?[1]

[1] Anna Q. T. Parsons.

To answer your question, — our morning potatoes are thus prepared. They are chopped up, having been previously boiled, mixed with milk, a little butter and salt and heated in the oven, and now that Mrs. Codman gets the breakfasts, we have it *first-rate*, — as well as the *brewis*.

Brisbane will be here again soon to stay a while, with Parke Godwin,[1] Osborne Macdaniel, etc. Wish you would come.

Now I hope, dear Anna, that all your creature comforts are attended to, and that you look "first rate," as we Brook Farmers say, in your new year, and that you will find time to write to me immediately. Tell my friends I yearn to be in Boston.

You have no idea, in La Grange Place, of the mysterious beauty of winter. Last night how magnificent! We walked on beds of diamonds, and diamonds blazed over our heads.

I'm so ashamed of this writing! — Am thankful Fred isn't here to see it. — Do burn up the letter. — Newcomb still stays away. — In haste and in love to you and yours

Mary Ann

Sunday a.m., Jan. 5, '45.

Dear Frank,

Have you not Rollin's *Ancient History?* and if you have, will you please to do it up, direct it to John Orvis, and leave it at Miss Peabody's? John has been wanting it for some time, and I have unfortunately forgotten to ask you for it, and he has thought of it, but would not mention it, for fear you wanted it.

[1] Parke Godwin was at this time assisting Bryant to edit the New York Evening Post.

I wish you were here today. It is bright and pleasant. I had a very pleasant ride out here, found Caroline Whitney in the stage. Thank you for my little book, which is very pretty. I've not had time to read any of it yet. Amelia is pleased with hers, — sends love, and any tender, sentimental speeches that you please to imagine, — is tired out today with last night's performances. *Pizarro*[1] went off finely — much better than I should have thought. I wish you had seen it. Don't think it will be repeated. The cost of time and trouble is too great. Elvira's performance was excellent. So were Pizarro, Bella and Cora — and particularly little Matilda Patterson, Cora's child. She looked like a little angel, and behaved beautifully. Perhaps the costumes formed the best part of the whole. — They were quite splendid. I don't see where they found time and materials for preparing them.

Shall I dare tell you that Frank Cabot says that the sun Amelia painted looked like a summer squash? . . .

In haste
Mary Ann

Jan. 6 — Monday eve, 1845.

Dearest Anna,

. . . Here I sit in Mrs. Whitehouse's room, having lately returned from Teachers' meeting — it is past ten o'clock — Amelia, John Dwight, J. Orvis, and Mrs. W. are playing cards (!)[2] Sarah[3] is sewing, and I, with soul as drear as the weather without, am cheering myself by writing

[1] Lindsay Swift says the performance was a failure.

[2] People were quite free to play cards at Brook Farm but they seem to have preferred almost any other form of amusement.

[3] Sarah Whitehouse.

to thee. You have heard Hudson's lecture tonight, should like to have listened with you. Fred has gone in to hear him with his sister Mary, and is now I suppose riding home in this dismal, dark night. Heaven cheer him! He came home this morning — told me that he saw you Sunday a.m. the last thing before he left Boston — I was glad to hear from you. And now to tell you what you wished me to write. — Sunday p.m. at half past three, I was at a meeting of the fancy group in this very room — and at half past nine in the evening, was here also. Martin and Sarah were here sound asleep, and I was dancing round to keep myself awake. — Did you find me? [1]

Newcomb isn't inclined to say much about the notes and I don't think he cares particularly to have you read more. He says there was one particular feeling he wished to see if you would get at. — He won't tell what, — but he says you had a shadow of it now and then. — I think he feels satisfied. — He says, tell her her dream is entirely true — with regard to the essay, etc. he says he has nothing to say, — only that that is *your* interpretation of it. He is ill today.

Oh! Anna, I wish you had the exquisitely beautiful flowers that are on my bureau — quite a large bouquet from our greenhouse [2] — roses and buds — a splendid carnation, heliotrope — geranium, myrtle, etc., etc. presented to me by Lucas. But for hurting Lucas's feelings, I would have sent them to you tonight by Fred.

What a delightful visit I had at your house — I can't tell you how much I enjoyed it. Tell Celia I gave her

[1] Miss Parsons wishes to test some impression of her own received at the precise times stated.

[2] The greenhouse, under the direction of Peter N. Kleinstrup, was a new feature at the Farm in the fall of 1844.

message and gift to Charles Dana today. — He was highly amused — says he shall have to write a poem to the unknown.

Good night, dearest friend, . . . good night. Come to me in dreams.

Mary Ann

Brook Farm, Jan. 8, '45.

Dear Frank,

We intended to have written you a good, long letter this evening, but have been to the Shakespeare reading at the Eyrie, and just returned now at eleven o'clock — found our fire out; — moreover last night slept but three or four hours. Mrs. Whitehouse intended to have left today for Baltimore, so invited a number of us to card-playing and a hot supper of roast potatoes. Mr. Ripley, Dana and John were present. It so happened that Eunice Macdaniel (it being her birthday) not knowing of this party invited the same set to drink hot chocolate with her, so we adjourned from one room to the other, and kept it up pretty late. They were very pleasant parties, or rather it was the same party. . . .

Your affectionate sister
Mary-Ann

P.S. I find some beautiful pieces in my little book.

(*Place your hand on the bottom of this, and the top of the next page and tell me what impression you get.*)

Tuesday eve, Jan. 14, 1845.

Dearest Anna,

. . . Mr. Newcomb is *very desirous* to have you send him the rest of your impressions, and if you will enclose them to me, and hand the package to Fred, it will probably come safe. I had a fine ride out here Sunday p.m. The roads were really *dazzling* with light, and right glad was I to be here on *some* accounts, tho' nothing could have pleased me better than to stay with you. The truth was (and I didn't tell you) that we were expecting an unusual and important meeting Sunday evening, from which I would not have been absent, if I could possibly have been present. You must not speak of what I am going to tell you. You know very well that we have a *few* discordant spirits here, — that they form a party (what a word for Association!) and have from time to time made mischief and are constantly undermining what the others are doing, — besides making things continually unpleasant. Well now, thank Heaven, affairs have come to [1] a crisis. It has been clearly ascertained that this troublesome party are a very small minority, perhaps about five or six individuals. All their cabalism, their narrowness, their meanness, has been clearly laid before them, by the founders of this institution, and Sunday evening the choice was given them to succumb, to come into harmony, — to cease their suspicions and mean slander, — or to quit us at once, and they were told that unless they did one of these two things, they would certainly be expelled. Knowing as I did, that all this was to come up that evening, do you wonder that I wished to be here? and knowing, as you must, that such meetings can't be particularly pleasant, however happy the result, you will now believe that I should have spent a more quiet and delightful time with you.

Since that evening Brook Farm atmosphere seems to me

[1] This is the bottom of the page, from which and from the top of the next, Miss Parsons is to get an impression.

clearer and brighter. I see nothing more to prevent us from getting along delightfully.

This evening we attend an oyster supper in Amelia's room, an altogether *aristocratic* party (!!) — the Danas, Macdaniels, Brisbane, Channing (the divine), Fred and Orvis, — Dwights, Hosmers, Ripleys, etc. How I wish you and Helen were to be with us!

Now when will you come? I don't know how long the gentlemen from New York will be here, probably thro' the week; and I don't know what is going to happen on any evening, but if you can come, I trust we may have a good time at any evening and I trust Helen will come with you. —

Oh dear! I keep thinking (selfishly — shall I ever be anything *but* selfish?) how lonely, how dismal it will be when Fred is gone to the Cottage. There I can't do him any good, — here there is some little trifle every day — and trifles, alas! they always did, they always will make my happiness. It is a fact. I *must cease to be happy*, — unless by help of Heaven I can become wholly unselfish. Do write to your true and loving friend

Mary Ann

Mr. Brisbane asked me to write him a letter of introduction to you.[1] I've concluded to stay at home and help, and not go to the convention.

[*Enclosure*]

Dearest Anna,

It gives me pleasure to introduce to you *Mr. Brisbane*, whose acquaintance I am sure you will be happy to make, You will find him much interested in Neurology.

Yours ever

Mary Anne

Brook Farm
Tuesday eve., Jan. 14.

[1] Anna Parsons's personal distinction was such that leading thinkers of the day sought introductions.

Jan. 15 a.m., 1845.

Dear Frank,

You will see a *host* of our people at the convention [1] today. Amelia, M. A. Ripley, Maria, John, Fred, Orvis, Eunice, etc., etc. *We* have concluded to stay here, and have what good time we may.

Tho' sorry to leave you last Sunday, I was glad to be here. I was expecting an important meeting in the evening, — and would not on any account have been absent. Matters have come to a crisis at last, thank Heaven; — and the *few* intriguing, caballing, mean, troublesome, people, have been very plainly dealt with, and told that if they don't go, or come into harmony, — wholly cease their caballing and their slander, they will be expelled! This is good, — *now* our atmosphere is bright and we shall go on finely.

Saturday evening, Rebecca Codman had a candy frolic to celebrate her birthday. They took away the tables from the dining hall, and danced there in their calico gowns and aprons and had a card-party in the kitchen. From all accounts they had a fine time.

How I *should* like to hear Channing! [2] Do be present at his speeches, if you can. . . .

In a hurry
Mary Ann

Brook Farm, Sunday, Jan. 19, 1845.

Dear Anna, dear friend,

Your letter [3] fills me with joy unspeakable, and encourages me to cherish more devotedly than ever the cause I have espoused. It is the cause of humanity, — the cause

[1] To spread the doctrines of Fourier. [2] At the convention.

[3] In which Anna Parsons tells her friend that she is completely a convert to associative principles.

of God. There is nothing small or partial in it, — nothing that ever can be outlived or outgrown so long as humanity lasts, and thank Heaven, nothing but what we do hope and expect to attain. The spirit of despair has spread her chilling wings over the world until now, — beneath their shadow, with tearful eyes, has man struggled to work out his destiny and reach a higher and happier life. Now Hope smiles in the clear blue sky, and Faith takes him by the hand to lead him through paths of joy, to a harmonious and blissful future. We are so ensnared, so beset with temptations, so tortured with trials, that we have made a virtue of necessity and preached up the need of *working* out our salvation by hard struggles with the enemy. How absurd! Look into your inner life. Did you ever feel that sorrow in itself gives you strength? Wasn't it rather an obstacle, an enemy, that, from some higher and happier source, some *hope* or *faith* or *joy* that was in you, you must draw strength to conquer? Have you not sometimes felt almost omnipotent from the impulse of some *joyful* emotion? What else has ever given you such strength? It seemed that love, or hope, or faith *alone* could conquer any obstacle. But I will not speak on this subject, when you have heard divine words from golden lips.[1]

I said your letter gave me joy — yes, — and because that divine man has kindled joy in your soul; — has given you a glimpse of the kingdom of heaven on earth, and furnished you with an object worth living for. I have mourned with you, that I could not see you filled with my

[1] The phrase "golden lips," a literal translation of the name of Saint Chrysostom, is used in Emerson's poem, *The Problem,* as a synonym for eloquence. It doubtless gets into Miss Dwight's vocabulary from this source. In this case the divine words were evidently Channing's.

childish (?) enthusiasm, because it is and has been to me the source of so much joy. Without it I could not have strength to lift a finger in the work of life. I would rather *die* than lose it. Deep down in my heart, — far in the background of my inner life — hangs a dark veil of sadness. It would take from me all power of action, if I were to allow myself to contemplate it; but thanks to the ardor and joy and enthusiasm of my being, it is able only to mingle a sober hue with the bright, prismatic rays that dance around me. Now you have an object to live for and I rejoice. I have seen that you scarcely felt that you belonged to us here on earth, and that you were willing to leave us at any time. Well, so perhaps you should be *willing*, — and also you should be *willing* and *happy* to *live*. Yes, — Association has *work* for you. Mourn not that hands and feet are tied;[1] we have work for *you*. The race is not always to the swift nor the battle to the strong. We need all the spiritual influence that can be brought to bear upon Association. If you have not hands and feet for us, you have a head and a heart to devote to our service, and it will be your joy and your life and strength to use them for Association. And if you cannot yet be here on the spot with us, — you will exert, you may depend upon it, a great deal of influence in your present sphere. Ask not how; it will be revealed to you at the moment what you shall say and do, if your spirit is earnest. Ah! Anna, we cannot live truly, until we have such devotion to some noble object or idea — that we could die for it.

I rejoice much in the convention. Fanny and I sat up Thursday evening to await the arrival of our people home from the convention. Mr. Brisbane and Macdaniel[2]

[1] By delicate health. [2] Osborne Macdaniel.

and the ladies of our house came at half past eleven — and we had a joyful meeting. They brought me your notes and a letter from Fred. We sat up till one having the merriest time, telling and hearing all about the convention, etc. Then came a wagonload of gentlemen, but we didn't sit up to see them any nearer home than the Hive. Mr. Brisbane told me he saw you and should see more of you when he goes to Boston again. What an intellect he has! But you needn't be afraid of him.

Oh, this day and yesterday! Was ever earth clad in such beauty? Would you were here to slide and coast over our hills of glistening white marble, — to admire the glittering coral branches that border our paths, and the trees of crystal, of silver and of diamonds, that make magnificent this fairy palace. Have I seen such beauty in a former existence, — or is it the realization of some dream or fancy? — that it continually *reminds* me of something, I know not what? Yesterday a.m. as soon as the sun came out I went into the Pine Woods with Fred. I had never seen nature in this pure crystal dress — and shall never forget it. We sat long on the wall that fronts the Pine Woods and looked at the dazzling, delicate beauty, and talked. In this walk Fred told me what Channing said of the superiority of joy to sorrow. In the afternoon a party of our people went. Today we have had grand coasting and still this beauty surrounds us; still we are in a magician's palace. Oh! that you could have come!

It is tea-time and I must away — but I go not away from thee. — All day you have been in my thot's — write soon, dear friend, to

Your affectionate
Mary-Ann

Friday evening, Jan. 24, [*1845.*]

I am alone and at leisure (!), dear Anna, and the few moments thus blessed shall be given to thee. The rain is beating against my window and I fear it will not be pleasant enough for Fanny to go to Boston tomorrow should there be a concert.

By and by we are to have some kind of a *scrape* at the Macdaniels' room. S. Whitehouse's room is turned into a kitchen for the *fixings*. What sort of a *soirée* can I get up, dear Anna? Anything for variety. Why have you not been to see me? Is it because Seth Welles is still on that jury? I expected you Wednesday and Thursday, the days were so magnificent. Six days we have been under enchantment. Today the spell is broken. — Never have I beheld — scarcely have I dreamed of such beauty. What thanks would I not have given to have had you by my side in my morning walks from the Hive to the Eyrie! Good heavens! What a prospect! The hills edged with such glittering white; — the distant woods like wreaths of white mist, — the nearer trees hung with glittering diamonds; — their winter fruits. I will not attempt to describe it, — put your hand here and see it, if you can.

Mrs. Ripley bro't your very welcome note, — you bless me every time you write. Mrs. Davis Weld came to see me last Monday and from her I learned what a furor pervades the saints [1] who are afraid to hear Parker. Heaven help them! for it is dark as Egypt around them. Such commotions always do good.

[2] A chosen body of our people are exceedingly busy

[1] The other Unitarian ministers (except of course William Henry Channing and the transcendentalists generally).

[2] A few lines have been quoted in Cooke's *John Sullivan Dwight.*

A PHALANSTERY AS PROJECTED BY FOURIER

making a new constitution.[1] I guess we shall have a good one, and such a one as will make civilizees [2] open their eyes wide with astonishment. I wish you could have seen, or could see the pictures Mr. Brisbane has of a Phalanstery [3] and its domain in full harmony. They are magnificent in design, and give one a pretty clear glance at least into the kingdom of heaven that is to come on earth. Mr. Brisbane and Mr. Macdaniel are still here. I like them very much. We have had some very pleasant social unions, some walks and glorious feasts. . . .

We have among new comers a Mr. Whittamore and a Mr. Curtis.[4] John, walking home from the woods, overheard between them this conversation. Mr. W. "The girls here are *pretty slick*." Mr. C. "Yes! a very good place for a fellow to come who wants to look him up a girl." They were very disinterested, — disclaimed all idea of wishing to be married, etc., etc. We've had a little rich fun out of this. A Mr. Peppercorn has come amongst us. John Orvis made us laugh last evening. His office is to provide strangers with beds. He declared he had planted the peppercorn in the wrong bed, and he had no doubt but he would be up the next morning! . . .

What a letter I must have written you the last time. It must have been more poor and fragmentary than usual and just because I had that to say which ought, could

[1] The new constitution of the Brook Farm Phalanx was adopted in March, 1845 and the Phalanx incorporated by the Legislature of Massachusetts on May 1.

[2] This word is anglicized from Fourier's "civilisés," the people living under the usual conditions of competitive industry.

[3] One of these is reproduced on the preceding page.

[4] It may be needless to say that this is neither Burrill nor George W. Curtis.

I have said it, to make a good letter. Would I were not ever in a hurry. — It is nine o'clock — time for the party — I must go, — and bid thee good night, sending thee with my own love, any quantity from my family and my neighbors. Write soon and come soon. Love to all.

Mary Ann

Thank you for the favor you did me with regard to Mr. Sumner and the lamp shades. He shall have some.

I have written to Frank to call and borrow for me some books of birds. Will you lend them?

Brook Farm, Sunday, Jan. 26, '45.

Dear Frank,

Amelia sits here with me in my room and says she is thinking of you. — I wish and have wished more than once today that you were here with us. I hope you bear your disappointment in not seeing Frances yesterday, as a good Christian ought, — it was too bad. How did you enjoy the concert? And did you go alone?

Mr. Brisbane and Mr. Macdaniel will leave us tomorrow a.m. and will be very much missed here. This forenoon Mr. B. gave us an Association sermon. It was very good, very excellent in matter, but rather dull inasmuch as it partook of the nature of a sermon. He says Christianity, till within a century or two, has been striking root in the earth; its manifestations have been inverse, shooting down like the roots of a tree, — now it is well rooted, and must henceforth shoot up in the true, divine order, — a very good idea.

I wish I could get some of Fourier's works for you. I am going to read *Le nouveau Monde industriel*, a copy of which belonging to Caroline Sturgis is now in John's possession. I have engaged to paint some lamp shades to send into Boston, and am really in want of those books of birds which Fanny Parsons once lent me. I want to paint some of them on the lamp shades and I want them as soon as I can possibly have them. If you will call there at once, and borrow a couple of volumes for me, and leave them at Miss Peabody's properly directed, you will confer a very great favor. Perhaps they will come out to me Monday or Tuesday. After the painting is finished, I varnish it with Mastic varnish — which renders it transparent, and the effect is very beautiful by lamp light. I should like to have you see them very much. Today I have been painting the little wreath for your watchcase which I promised you so long ago, and am sorry not to have sent to you sooner. You must come out next Saturday and have it. . . .

I don't know that much has happened to us this week. Fred, I believe, has decided not to go to Boston, which, of course, is well for us. Oh! yes there *has* been important work done this week. A dozen chosen ones have been busy all day and thro' the evening, making a new constitution for us, and the work is done. I trust it is a good one. Our association is to be called the "Brook Farm Phalanx." John Allen [1] has visited us this week — and has concluded to come and join us next March, and then the Phalanx and his paper, the Social Reformer, are to be united in one, called the Phalanx and printed here.

What a day we had last Sunday and what a scene of en-

[1] The Reverend John Allen, a Universalist minister, had left his church because he did not feel free to speak from the pulpit against slavery. He became an important member of Brook Farm. A little later he and John Orvis lectured for the cause throughout New England and New York.

chantment! — and it lasted till the next Friday morning. Perhaps I have never enjoyed so much the beauty in the landscape. The morning walks from the Hive to the Eyrie are never to be forgotten.

Fanny says the Graham crackers are excellent. . . . Amelia had a coffee party again this evening — and now farewell.

Your affectionate sister
Mary-Ann

Brook Farm, Monday, Jan. 27, 1845.

Dear Frank,[1]

My whole soul is awake this beautiful, spring-feeling day and I cannot resist stealing time to write and tell you about last evening. — O — O — O — Oh! Cannot you almost hear me sigh for a little leisure, — sweet leisure to spend with you and others whom I love? But now several important things claim this very hour which I give you, yet I obey the divine impulse and must write, tho' in haste. I hope you have received today a note from me. I mentioned therein Amelia's coffee party. She did not *call* it a party either. There were Mr. Brisbane, Osborne Mac., Fanny and Eunice Mac., Mr. Ripley, Mr. Dana, M. A. Ripley, Maria, Sarah Whitehouse, John Orvis, Fred C., J. S. Dwight, your sisters and last, not least *Amelia* — just fifteen of us. How differently matters often turn out from what we expect, and how often are we agreeably disappointed! So it happened at this memorable coffee party. J. Orvis came into my room with the headache, — I also had a dull headache. We spoke of the party — concluded we didn't care to go, — expected a stupid time, etc. In came Amelia to hurry us

[1] This letter has been quoted in Cooke's *John Sullivan Dwight.*

off — so we went. Coffee was handed round, — a few puns perpetrated, etc. — Meanwhile a holy inspiration from high heaven was stealing quietly and unseen over the souls of all present. The spirits of good angels and all lovers of humanity were gathering around us, — the soul of Fourier must have bent lovingly over the heads of our little band. Light and love, or the light of love began to beam from all eyes. Mr. Ripley proposed for a toast, "Albert Brisbane, the first apostle of Fourierism in our country", etc., — and made some interesting and rather humorous remarks about the great assistance he had afforded us in the convention, in the framing of the new constitution, etc., etc. Mr. B. disdained it all, grew eloquent in reply — spoke of B. Farm society, and the friendships he had enjoyed here, — the pleasure of receiving many kind offices from the hand of friendship, etc., etc. I cannot attempt to repeat the toasts that were given, they were so numerous and all good, — nor the excellent remarks that were made by Mr. Ripley, Mr. Dana, Mr. Brisbane and our brother. — Suffice it to say that I never heard either of them speak better. It was all beauty and inspiration, — there was true humor, eloquence, elegance, deep earnestness and sacred solemnity. After those present were toasted, beautiful tributes were paid to the absent. Fourier, William H. Channing — the priest and poet of Association — Greeley and other New York friends were remembered, and each toast prefaced by interesting remarks. Charles Dana proposed his friend, Parke Godwin — spoke of him with deep feeling and all the earnestness of affection, and just as he was concluding, Fred added, "*God wins* always in the end." So appropriate and good a pun was universally applauded. We set it down for Fred's best, — but afterwards found that he also was encircled with a heavenly halo, and everything he did that evening was his best. As the speeches became higher and holier and more beautiful and the broadest principles were uttered from golden lips, and our emotions grew more elevated and solemn, partaking of the highest aspirations of which the human soul is capable, Charles Dana spoke of a meeting in New York where they all joined hands and pledged themselves to the cause of Association, — and he called upon us warmly and fervently to do the same. With one impulse we all arose and formed a circle around the little table and hand in hand we vowed "*truth to the cause of God and humanity*." It was a solemn moment, never to be forgotten. Then our circle of friendship was toasted, — and then what beautiful allusions John made to our circle! and to circles within circles, — showing that this was no exclusive circle, that endless circles might be drawn around it, all having the same centre. Then Mr. Ripley wished very humorously that our Phalanx might grow till we could join hands all around Palmer's woods, round Cow Island, across the river, etc., etc. — Then Mr. Brisbane would have the circle surround the globe. Then Mr. Brisbane, after Mr. Ripley had been speaking of circles, said he had omitted the *ellipse*, (the emblem of love, centre in two foci) and made beautiful remarks upon that. Then John made a good pun, saying Mr. B. had supplied the *ellipse* (or omission) in Mr. R's speech. John toasted the coffee pot in this wise — "Our patient friend, the coffee pot. Tho' drained of its *contents*, it has not lost its patience, — if it is not *spiritual*, it certainly is not *material*" (is immaterial). Mr. Ripley jumped a foot and turned directly round at so good a pun. Fred gave a toast with no little wit and humor, "*John Allen!*

May his wisdom grow in his love." (Immense applause.) John gave a beautiful toast to the memory of the dead, — the dead moon, and all the events in the dead past which have led us on to possess any real life. I wish I could remember every word, it was so poetic and beautiful. Allusion had been made to Mr. Orvis (a pun) as Orpheus, John ending with saying, "God bless the sun and also Orpheus. God bless the moon and also Morpheus." Mr. Ripley made quite a long and humorous speech upon the glass of punch, quintessent punch, which he drank at a N. Y. meeting and which roused a dull company into great activity, — said it was so exquisitely compounded that if it had made a man quite drunk, it couldn't have injured his intellect. This called out two puns. John asked if the party was a punch and judy spree (jeu d'esprit) and Fred said, that it seemed only necessary to punch Mr. Ripley to get a good speech from him. . . .

At the breaking up Mr. Brisbane made some remarks about going to propagate the doctrine in N. Y., the city of frauds, etc., etc., — whereat in conclusion, Fred wished he might go his proper gait (propagate) and that the greatest fraud of which New York was guilty might be that of defrauding us of his presence. — So it ended at twelve o'clock, and we separated to pass sleepless nights, in the company of solemn, pleasing and exciting thoughts. Oh! Frank, had you been here! How I longed for you and Anna, and for mother!

Well, I can't spare time to write more, — I should like to have you lend this to Anna and Helen to read, as I am not able to write them. You must all imagine a great deal, I have described so poorly! You see our entertainment was a regular series, ascending gradually from a few jokes to the highest spiritual emotions, and then gradually descending again. I forgot to speak of Orvis, I forget his toast, — but he said beautiful things about the occasion and about Fourier, with whose spirit he felt that he had been holding communion. Write soon.

Your affectionate sister
Mary Ann

P.S. Monday evening. Your note to Fanny and me has just come. Tell Newhall, Father is very anxious to have the piano tuned as soon as possible.

Brook Farm, Thursday eve, Feb. 6, '45.

Dear Frank,

'Tis past 10 o'clock. We have just returned from the meeting (I mean an Association meeting to discuss the constitution, a very good meeting too). Of course, at this late hour I can't write much, but Fanny has been writing. We have been for a few days quite blocked up with snow. The day before yesterday we had a storm indeed. I never saw the like. Like a goose, I set off alone to go down to the Hive to set tables, — had exceeding difficulty in getting there, — found Eunice, who had come down with Charles Dana.

After tea John came down on purpose to insist that Eunice and I should stay all night, — said it was perfectly absurd for us to try to go home — we should be buried up, etc., etc. This was all nonsense of course, — I was determined to go, and would not be persuaded to stay. Eunice decided to stay, — so John and I set out. We waded all the way thro' deep snow, frequently almost up to my neck. The wind was blowing strange, dark symphonies the while, and

I assure you that, spite of the fatigue, there was something to enjoy in all this. We astonished the people when we reached the house. Fred seemed to regret very much that he had not gone down after me, for, he said, he could have carried me in his arms. He had taken it for granted I should sleep at the Hive. Up came Mr. Ryckman to the Pilgrim House, so that he might say he had been out in the storm. Then Fred tho't he would try it, so down he went to the Hive, and brought Eunice home, taking her in his arms thro' the deepest banks. I have some cold, but have felt the effects of the weather and my journey to and fro but very little. That same evening Salisbury was on his way home with a load of coal. Orvis took a team with two oxen and benevolently set off to meet him, took a different road, went nearly five miles and back again, and then overtook him at our bridge, where he had got fastened in the snow.

I should have written you sooner, but we have been blocked up, as I said, and could not get to Boston.

Jonathan B. Field [1] has come back, looking as handsome as ever.

In haste, good night.

Your affectionate sister
Mary Ann

Brook Farm, Sat. a.m., Feb. 15, '45.

Dear Frank,

I have been hoping all the week to get a letter from you, and to find time to write to you, but have been disappointed in both. I have given my chief attention this week to the lamp shades, have painted nine, and today I mean to rest

[1] Whose real name was Butterfield.

or rather to vary my occupation. . . . Fred sent you a letter this morning, and I believe he has sent you a copy of the Phalanx. I will send you, by the first opportunity, several numbers, that you may give them away, as we would be glad to have them distributed, — we want to send them to everybody we can think of. The arrangements are all settled for having it published here. It will require five hundred dollars to get a new printing press, and set the whole a-going, and Mr. Allen gives four hundred and Mr. Treadwell,[1] one. Then the N. Y. friends are exerting themselves to procure means of having a great publishing establishment here. $5000 are desirable for this, and $1000 are already procured. They write with much hope of success. A part of Mr. Shaw's investment will go to build a black-smith's shop directly, and part of it goes to buy block tin for Mr. Capen's business, who can find ready sale for any quantity of articles which he can manufacture. We are just about presenting to the government a petition to grant us a charter. Charles Sumner is going to make a strong statement in favor of it, and the probability is it will be granted.

Our new constitution is still under discussion. No doubt in my mind but it is a good one, yet John has brought forward a plan for government (which is rather no government but a simple organization) which recommends itself to me so strongly that I shall not easily be satisfied with anything else. He does not consider it a theory or plan of his own, but a regular deduction from Fourier's science, into which he is looking (Mrs. Ripley thinks) more deeply than any person here. It seems to me very perfect and simple and

[1] Treadwell and Butterfield did the printing for the Harbinger, the first number of which was issued at Brook Farm on June 14, 1845.

beautiful, but I cannot explain it here. Its chief merit consists in having the acknowledged practical heads of the different departments represent their departments in the general council or agency. They grow up, as it were, naturally to their offices, instead of being elected. I think the plan is liked, but the committee thought the time had not yet come for it; tho' perfect, it is not, in their opinion, practicable. John explained it to the Association at our last meeting, tho' not with the fulness and minuteness with which he intends to do so, and Charles Dana objected on the same ground as before and also on that of its not being scientific. He has not yet said wherein he thinks it impracticable or unscientific. Of course John would be glad to hear this, as he only presents his statement on the ground of science. He lay awake one night, when the thought first struck him, and studied it out. I did not like Charles D.'s manner. It was as if he had said to John, — You have presented this to the committee before, — *I* then examined into it, — *I* did not think it practical or scientific and now I don't wish to hear any more about it. Mr. Ryckman requested that John would write it off, that he might *see* it. He said he wished to know whether he felt strongly attracted to it from any real merit of its own, or from the beauty of the speech. The speech was a perfectly plain, unadorned, simple statement, — its beauty was in its simplicity, — when he has written it out, you must see it. I am afraid I cannot now get for you *The New Industrial World*,[1] with which I get on slowly. It is quite in demand here, and John says Charles Dana would have to be consulted.

[1] Fourier's most important work, which Mary Ann Dwight was reading in French.

Fred is almost ready to move to the Cottage, — and last evening, in honor of his departure, treated us to cake and coffee in Amelia's room. It was not a very spirited party tho'! Fred did his best, but the jokes wouldn't go, — from the Archon [1] we couldn't get a word. However, between eleven and twelve people grew quite lively. The best part of the entertainment was hearing Amelia recite *The Lady of Shalott* and some other poems. I don't like the thought of Fred's going to the Cottage, — shall miss him in a thousand ways.

Well now, I have written you quite a matter of fact letter and I wish you had it — fear you will not get it today. . . . I shall send some numbers of the Phalanx to Miss Peabody, and now fare thee well.

Thy affectionate sister
Marianne

P.S. *Sunday p.m.*

. . . Please distribute these numbers of the Phalanx thus — Anna Whitney's I've directed. Will you direct one to Uncle Dwight and send it, one to Isaac Osgood, to Eben Mann, to Harriet Graupner, one to Anna for Lucy Goddard, Davis Weld, Miss Gale, and to Mrs. Martin unless you prefer sending it somewhere else, and do as you please with the others. If I have not left you as many as you want, you can take D. Weld's or L. Goddard's.

Mary Ann

Brook Farm. — Thursday evening, Feb. 27, [*1845*].

Dearest Anna,

'Tis half-past ten o'clock. . . . I write from the solitude of my home; — we've had a music party at the Eyrie, —

[1] "The Archon" was Theodore Parker's name for his friend Ripley.

Fanny has not yet returned; — I left Fred at the Eyrie steps and sent him to his home at the Cottage, almost sick and looking as sober as if the spirits within were of the deepest blue.

Was my note to you solemncolly? I did not mean it should be. Indeed it was so much brighter than I felt at the time that I tho't it quite cheerful. Thank you for your kind words. They are in a measure true, and more true for some natures than they are for mine. When one is working for humanity, it is true that individual trials are lightened and lost sight of, — but here would be my trouble. I am ever seeking sympathy. When I find it, it makes all difficulties naught, all work a healthful pleasure, — but unless the sympathies of my nature are answered, I am paralyzed — I can do nothing. I always find that just so far as these sympathies are fully responded to, I can work, and no further. It seems a necessary condition to any healthy action, and it is one that, considering the subversive state of everything, has been as well supplied as could reasonably have been expected.

I keep very busy, painting six or seven hours a day — hence the shortness of my notes, — when not painting, I must rest my eyes. I have more demands for lamp shades and other painted fancy things than I can at present supply. I seem to have got myself into business at present. — I wish you were here to read to me when I sit alone in my room hour after hour, (and oh! how lonely I am lately, would you believe it?) . . .

Mr. Brisbane will be here in a few days. The executive committee in New York have had a meeting (don't speak of it at present) and decided that these three things must be done: 1st, The cause must be propagated thro' the Phalanx to be published here; 2d, Thro' lecturers to *scour* the country, and the funds will undoubtedly be raised to support Mr. Channing, Mr. Brisbane and Mr. Ripley on such a mission. (I don't know that Mr. Ripley can go); and thirdly, an appeal must be made to the citizens of the United States, who are interested in Association, and to the friends of the cause in Europe, to unite in raising funds for the carrying out of the experiment at Brook Farm.

C. K. N. is quite ill with sore throat, and other effects of a cold. Almost everybody has a cold. We are almost flooded here — never was there such walking — I doubt if you ever experienced the like in *mud* and *slosh* when you went to visit your sea-street acquaintances. Tell Frank, Mr. Dana wrote the letter in the Phalanx to an imaginary friend, — and Mrs. Sloan, the notice of M. A. Williams. How it came to be printed I don't know. Would you believe, I have not had time to read a word of the Phalanx yet!

A group has been organized for superintending amusements. Miss Russell, Maria, John, Eunice, Fanny, etc. I hadn't time to be present, but they voted me in, to take care of the decorations, etc., etc. — Now, dear, do write. Ever with love to you and yours

Marianne

I've given up the thought of going in to the concert tomorrow partly on account of weather and bad travelling.

M. A. D.

Sunday p.m., [*March 2, 1845*].

Dearest Anna,

I've just sent for Amelia and Orvis to meet mother, Fanny and myself in my room to hear John's constitution [1]

[1] Before submitting it to vote that same evening.

read — wish you were to be of the number; meantime I commence writing. Fred has gone to Boston to see Mary again before she goes to Hingham — God bless them. I certainly would have written to you sooner if I had had time — always the same excuse. Your letter is very interesting. Newcomb says he is willing to have you write off those notes for Emerson, — and you need not be sorry that you sent that paper to him. He told me, when he read it, to tell you that he was filled with wonder, and he seemed very much affected, Anna, by the reading thereof — seemed sober, dejected and I thought, pained; but he would not own that he felt so.

Yes, Anna dear, cousin Nelly's death was beautiful, — but sad and heart-rending to the afflicted family. I had a beautiful dream the night after I heard of it, — was anxiously watching a beautiful chrysalis, when all at once it floated gently up into the heavenly perfumed air, amid roses and flowers and in the clear sunlight a most delicate, silver net work (its prison house) fell from it and it changed into a beautiful butterfly as it soared aloft.

I am getting reconciled to the loss of my neighbors, they have a so much larger and pleasanter room, and Fred is a very angel of kindness to me, and will ever be one of my best friends. I have told Mary that she must not be jealous and I presume she knows well that she need not.[1]

I am very happy and joyful of late — finding my happiness as I often do in friendship. Perhaps these beautiful spring days affect me, — the morning air is balmy and sweet, and the birds are beginning to sing, and even the mud has dried up somewhat. I wish you could accompany me in my daily visit to the green house; you have hardly

[1] Fred Cabot has just broken the news of his engagement to Mary Lincoln.

an idea how beautiful it is. If it were only to inhale the fragrance it were worth while to step in there. Mr. Kleinstrup is a man of most exquisite taste. I am writing you a most flighty note — can't tell why it is, but I cannot catch the ideas I would communicate to you. It has been my desire for several days to write and I have much to say, but every thought vanishes strangely ere I can possibly put it on paper. — How sorry I am! You must put up with the best I can do, and I will try again soon. — The fact is I have been under some excitement of feeling for a day or two past — a pleasant excitement I can't very well write about now, and perhaps it is this which puts my ideas to such rapid flight.[1] Tonight we have another constitution meeting.

I told you about the R.L.S.G. (or rejected lover's sympathising group), did I not? Well you can't think how amusing it was, a day or two ago, to hear Charles Dana announce gravely at table, a meeting of the R.L.S.G. to be held at half past ten that evening, in the nursery, a punctual attendance required from all the members and from all those candidates for admission who were expected ere long to become members, — and no one to be admitted without the usual badges — and measures were to be taken for the admission of honorary members. All this was said off very solemnly and created not a little fun and enquiry.

If you know of any good new thing or old thing by way of amusement, please send me word. Remember I belong to the *Concordia*, or group for superintending amusements.

It was really too bad that you should have lost Mr.

[1] Fred Cabot's engagement has caused Marianne to examine her own state of feeling toward him. She discovers, somewhat to her surprise, that she is really more interested in some one else.

Emerson's call or calls. (Did you lose both?) If you can't make out my notes, send them to me to write for you. . . .

I owed Mary Lincoln an answer to two letters and had not written to her for some time, so today I wrote her quite a long letter. You deserve better than this, but you see I am not in the mood for talking to you as I would, and I have given you enough of nonsense, — so with love to thee and thine, farewell. When are you coming?

Mary Ann

May I ask of you the favor to lend me Miss Fuller's new work [1] just long enough for perusal after you have done with it yourself?

Sunday evening, March 9, [1845].

My dear Anna,

How pleasant and comfortable it is here in my little room this evening, and how clean, for I've had the carpet shaken, windows and paint washed, and I do wish you were here with me. I have not been out of the house and scarcely out of the room today, having a very severe head cold, and a strong tendency to ear-ache. I'll tell you how I've passed the day. Mother came up early and brought my breakfast. Then I had just put the room to rights, and sat down, when Fred knocked. . . . After talking awhile, Fred read to me, and thus the whole forenoon passed off, varied only with a call from Amelia and one from M. A. Willard. I was at work, whenever I felt able, painting a picture frame of white wood for Fred.[2] The subject is Pegasus in the stable, drawn by Anna Philbric, and I have surrounded it with a wreath of oak and laurel leaves, with acorns and berries. How I

[1] *Summer on the Lakes*, published late in 1844.

[2] An engagement present (?).

love to be at work for a dear friend! — this occupation has made the whole day pleasant to me. Then came my dinner, then a visit from M. A. Willard (whom I like very much, and who is visiting here) also a visit from John Cheever, who gets attracted here by the *fine arts!* (I hope Dora won't be *jealous*.) They stayed till about tea time. John Cheever brought up my supper, and stayed talking on high and sublime subjects till the present time, and now again I am alone. George Curtis has been here a few days, is now at the Eyrie singing, and were I not afraid to go out I should not now be writing to thee.

Colds are very prevalent here now. Eunice is quite ill — poor thing! She has been made a mummy of, — done up in a wet sheet, — which she thinks a very unpoetical way of getting cured. Brisbane is here, but I scarcely see him. Indeed I'm so busy at my painting that I scarcely see any one, — and I assure you I feel very happy to have such profitable work to do. I have made some improvements in the shades.

I don't know how I feel about Fred and Mary, — glad and happy when I think of them, and yet not wholly confident. There is always in the future so much less of happiness, than is anticipated by these ecstatic lovers. I cannot think of Fred as married, — and *belonging* to any *one*. I don't like to think of myself in the matter at all, and I ought not, but this is human weakness — and I can't help fearing, that, for a while at least he must belong less to *me* than he has done. But I will not contemplate losing so good a friend, — no, — heaven sent him to be my help and strength, — and we have had, and must continue to have no little influence upon each other. Certainly now he is very kind and as friendly as ever. Why do people foolishly want to marry? I am getting to think that Fourier is right, and in full harmony there will be no marriage — at least marriage will be a very different thing from what it now is. Heaven grant that this may be the blessedest thing for Fred! If it prove so, then I am sure I shall feel happy, — for he deserves well. But if the sun of his early and promising life be dimmed, then I am sure I shall feel the shadow. I do trust that this most important step of his life is a right one, — but then he is so young! Oh! it would be sad to be disappointed in him, and I know I shall not be; he must find in Mary his truest help in his onward path. God speed him! I cannot imagine anything that I could not cheerfully sacrifice for his highest good and happiness. . . .

Good-night, dear friend.

Thine in love
Marianne

Wed. a.m., March 19, 1845.

Dear Frank,

. . . We are getting dreadfully crowded again. A whole tribe of carpenters have come to work on the Phalanstery, — and we have a gardener and his wife, and visitors, — and beds and table seats are quite in demand again. . . . Did you get mother's note?

As soon as we can get another place Miss Peabody's will cease to be our depot. — They are tired of the trouble. . . .

In all love
Mary Ann

B. Farm, Sunday, March 30, 1845.

Dear Frank,

. . . Today we have had two lectures on Phonography[1] from Mr. Boyle, who is giving a course (I didn't

[1] Boyle's system of phonography, or short hand.

hear them, by the way) and one from Mr. Kreutzer which I did hear, and was much amused and instructed. I like the man much. We had another Hive dance on Thursday evening, in honor of the bride, Mrs. Sawyer — and on the 7th of April we hope to have a *glorious time*, and *you must* and *shall* come. — John says you will, and nothing I trust, will prevent.

Fred lives at the street, — we hardly see him at all, and he is as good as dead to us just now. By a new arrangement we Grahamites [1] take all our meals at second table, so here I sit writing to you whilst all are off at tea. I hope another arrangement will soon fix it otherwise. My lamp shades continue in great demand. Mrs. Ripley yesterday received one dollar apiece. If you and I were acquainted with Phonography, I would have written you a long letter in the time I have given to this. Amelia sends her "particular" love to you — is painting landscapes on lamp shades, and succeeds very well.

If you go by Sumner's you will see some of the handsomest I have made — new patterns. . . . Do write very soon. We don't send things to Miss Peabody's now, and have no place, but anything left at Brown and Hastings, corner Warren St., will come. Good-bye.

Mary Ann

Pilgrim House, Tuesday, a.m., April 8, '45.

Dear Anna,

I will not say aught of our disappointment that you and Helen were not with us last evening, for I know that you were here in the spirit, and would have rejoiced to have

[1] Grahamites were vegetarians and ate bread made of unbolted (Graham) flour, according to the principles of Sylvester Graham, the dietician.

shared with us the wealth of those hours, had it been a possible thing and the best thing for you to have done so. Away then with regrets and let me, in my feeble way, tell you something of our celebration of the birthday of Fourier. Perhaps you may discover the secret by which, with no means and no time for preparation, we really produced a very beautiful and inspiring effect. You would hardly have believed yourself in our old, smoky Hive. Enter the dining hall at the farthest door (near the kitchen), and you will find yourself by some magic, in an illumined garden. Evergreens and beautiful greenhouse plants in full bloom delight your eye; there are roses and jasmines surmounted by the stately calla, the emblem of unity, and around that pillar, at the head of the table, the multiflora has twined its sweet blossoms. The tables are towards the centre of the hall, in the form of a cross, and elegantly adorned with bread and fruit and flowers. Before you, at the farthest end of the hall, gracefully bestowed across the windows, hangs our unitary banner, striped with the primary colors, and edged with white. In the centre of this, upon a pure azure background, are arranged in a semi-circle the words, "Universal Unity," in purest white, glittering, silver letters. This was the work and idea of Fanny Macdaniel, and was most beautifully executed; every letter is perfect; you must see it some day. In front of this stood the piano. — Turn round now, and look at the opposite end of the room. Across the wall in largest letters of evergreen, you read FOURIER 1772, an anchor at the left, and a bee hive, surrounded by bees, at the right. On a table in front is a bust of Charles Fourier, taken after his death. We intended to have thrown the seven colors upon this, with a prism, but it was *no go* by lamp light. I ought to have said the evergreen letters and emblems were the work of William Cheswell, one of our carpenters, and tho' beautiful in itself, it seemed doubly beautiful, coming from such a source, and was put there by him, to surprise us all before any other decorations were made, or scarcely thought of. Look now at the sides of the room. Between the windows in the centre, upon a black ground, hung a white lyre with seven strings of the seven rainbow colors. This gave us the unity of sound. This was John's idea and was roughly executed by me. Opposite in evergreen letters you read this motto, which I selected and executed: "But the Comforter, who is the Holy Spirit, whom the Father will send in my name, — He shall teach you all things and bring all things to your remembrance whatsoever I have said unto you." During the speeches, in allusion to this motto was given, "Fourier, the second coming of Christ." Near this you read, "Les attractions sont proportionnelles aux destinées."[1] The whole scene was beautiful; as John Allen said this morning, it was, together with the speeches, something that could not be put upon paper.

Thursday a.m. Oh! the *dissipation* of this Brook Farm life! Here is your letter not finished yet. Tuesday evening I was sleepy enough to go to bed as soon as our Association meeting was over, and last night, another small party, — a farewell to Mr. Brisbane, who leaves us today and leaves a void here that must be felt until his return, which he says, will be when he can come like a dove, with wings tipped with gold. Fred "hoped that if he came like a dove,

[1] The quotation represents Fourier's doctrine of "passional attraction," that each person is divinely attracted towards the work and the persons that are properly his.

CHARLES FOURIER

Under whose influence the Brook Farmers tried to form a Phalanx.

he would bring golden eagles with him, whose bills would all be bank bills, and whose notes, notes of hand." Our party last evening broke up when "we were at *one*" (o'clock), as the same Fred significantly said. A deep sadness gave a tone to all the conversation, yet the whole was most cheering and encouraging; as John said, we felt by what an ocean of joy and beauty we are surrounded, that we are able to bear the deep tragedy that must be going on in the soul, when one is living for a great idea. Much was said of the suffering, — the inward untold suffering — of the pioneers of this movement, — and Mr. Ripley said we had best *own* it, meet it strongly, and care nothing about it, — our individualities must be forgotten; or rather, as unity itself without individuality would be tame, we must put up with the evil and suffering attendant upon this transition state, and keep alive our faith and hope that it will be but temporary. Here shines the beauty of Mr. Brisbane's character. He is lost in the cause to which he is devoted, and in which he lives. His relations with us are of the most impersonal character; so sweet and sad is he, so full of feeling and entire devotion to the cause of God and humanity, that he has won our hearts. The inward experience that the speakers revealed last evening corresponded well with mine, — more of suffering and more of joy in this Brook Farm life, than could be summed up in all my previous life. Fred said somewhat to which all our hearts responded, about the happiness we enjoy, — that he would not exchange a day here for a year in civilization. I said all responded, — no, Mr. B. suggested (as Mary sat by his side) that Fred rather overstated — he thought there must be something individual in his happiness.

Well, now to go back to the Fourier celebration — I can't tell you about those speeches. They were great and good, and relieved by various songs. Mr. Ripley never was so happy and so great. His humor was unequaled. Dana, Brisbane, John D., Orvis, Allen, Frank Shaw and others were exceedingly interesting. John D. was speaking of Ambition (of its true development according to Fourier), and told how he had always despised this passion, — so much so that when he went to college he used to miss his lessons on purpose. "But now," said he, "I confess, by Heaven, I am ambitious. I would be omniarch of the globe." You can't think how rich this was, coming out, as it did, in the most natural, I-don't-care way. The silver white motto gave a tone to the evening, and the highest passion, unity, pervaded every soul. But enough, I can do no justice to it, and may as well stop here.

And now to go back an evening further, — to Sunday evening. We had then a great lecture from Mr. B. on the origin of evil. He traces it to three causes; matter, transition, and individuality; and gave the only satisfactory explanation I have ever heard.

Did you get Fred's letter? I hope you'll mind him, for you must not, for a long time, try your impressibility. And now I have a request to make, and I expect your mother and father and all will say ay to it, because your health requires it. You must come out here directly and make me a visit. I wish you could prevail on the powers to sanction your coming here to board this summer, and perhaps, if you come out and stay a week or two with me, they will let you keep on staying, or come again soon. . . .

This sitting up late will never do for me, — how weak and miserable my head feels! We are all good for nothing today. Many send love to you, dear friend, and join me in the wish to see you here. Will you come?

Adieu
Mary Anne

P.S. I must not omit to tell you that last evening, when Brisbane became speculative, he talked of our meeting 35000 years hence under Saturn's ring; and we agreed to do so! 35000 years from that very evening.

Wed. evening, April 30, '45.

Dear Frank,

It is bedtime and I am getting tired and sleepy, but will keep my eyes open long enough to say a few words to you. — This is a busy time. Our old constitution dies tonight, and tomorrow we commence life under a new charter. How will it work? This is a great and momentous question with us. I look for much good, — but we so lack the means necessary for perfecting any arrangements. Why we have scarcely a perfect group on the place, for want of more people. Still, it is interesting to watch these little beginnings. They are like the good seed in which we see in miniature the whole tree. How I wish people had more faith! With more truthfulness and wisdom I think we should have, — but now it dies out of the heart too often. I've just been talking with Amelia, who is in a most distrustful mood, and all from personal considerations. I sometimes feel that she will get tempted back into civilization ere long, she is so little satisfied with her actual state here. We have been organizing groups today preparatory to the change we make tomorrow. . . .

It is out of the question to get the epigæa[1] now, is it not?

[1] Trailing arbutus.

I wish it could be had. — John brought me from Mr. Follen's a set of wild flowers painted by a Mrs. Webber. — The whole arrangement is beautiful and many of the flowers very well done. — I long to be at work at this.[1] I've just been making a beautiful fan for the fancy group, hoping to find it a salable article.

What beautiful mornings we've had, and what awful, horrible, cold face-ache-giving afternoons! What's in the weather? Have you seen Anna? And how is she? and what have you to tell us? Write soon, and now good-night.

Affectionately
Mary Ann

Pilgrim House, Sunday p.m., May ? [*1845*].

My dear friend,[2]

. . . Today I have wished for you to enjoy with us a most delightful visit from Robert Owen. Never was I so agreeably disappointed in any one. The old man has a beautiful spirit, of infinite benevolence, — I really love and reverence him. He is 74, full of energy and activity, very courteous, attends carefully to every little etiquette, pats the children on the head and has a smile and a pleasant word for all. Last evening he gave us a lecture on socialism and another today. I'm astonished at his views, to find that we differ much in speculations and in details, yet we have one and the same object, and can meet on common ground. After his lecture he gave us an account of his experiment at New Lanark which he carried on with 2000

[1] Marianne Dwight painted perhaps a hundred pictures of wild flowers on large cardboard sheets. They are very accurate in drawing and coloring and I am assured by a young artist of the most modern school that my impression of their high artistic worth is entirely justified.

[2] This letter is quoted in G. W. Cooke's *John Sullivan Dwight.*

persons for 30 years, and then left in the care of others. These people were of the very dregs of society when he took them, — now they are mentioned in statistics, as being the most moral population of Great Britain. The whole story was very interesting, — so was his account of the Rapp community. I have always associated his name with New Harmony, but he says this was conducted by people who understood not his principles. After he had finished, Mr. Ripley rose and paid him a very handsome tribute, inviting him to be with us whenever he could, and expressing our sense of the honor we felt he had conferred upon us — proposed "Robert Owen," as a sentiment, wishing he might always enjoy in his own mind that sublime happiness that will one day be the portion of the human race. I wish I could see you and tell you of this interesting forenoon. He expressed himself much pleased with our experiment, and wondered at our success — is going to England, to return here in September. *He* has taken the common sense path to Association.

I've been having with mother and Frank a delightful little walk in the woods, gathered the first wild flowers, anemones and white violets, with the intention of sending them to you, but as their delicacy made me fear they would wither before you could get them, and as Sarah Whitehouse almost fell into ecstasies over them, I gave them to her.

I've been enjoying everything very much now these few days. I feel the beauty that I have hitherto only seen around me. The whole burden is removed from my soul, — my spirits are elastic and joyous.[1] . . .

[1] The rest of this letter is missing.

Wed. eve., May 14, [*1845*].

My dear Anna,

'Tis out of the question to write you any but a few hurried lines now, for my eyes will be too weak to paint tomorrow unless I give them a rest. Last evening we had a remarkably pleasant time at a small party (an extemporaneous party) given by John to celebrate his birthday. Mr. Ripley was brilliant, and so were our other friends. Dr. Brisbane,[1] the one who emancipated his slaves, from Cincinnati, was with us, also his wife, and Mr. Thornbury from Ohio Phalanx. Oh! that you could be with us on these occasions — we do live in an atmosphere of our own, and it is so inspiring, so ennobling! Whenever we meet, we breathe the spirit of universal unity; we assemble, as it were, around the altar of unity, and this gives a tone to all our communings. Even Dr. Brisbane felt it, and said he must be excused from making a speech, for tho' he felt deeply moved and gratified, he found himself in a new world, and should have to learn a new language first. And now for the important part of my note. — Channing, Brisbane, Godwin and Greeley are coming here the last of May to stay a few days, and we intend to have a first of June celebration in the Pine Woods (on some pleasant day thereabouts), and I wish you would see Mr. Welles, and ask him for me to bring you and Helen out here with him, as you will all enjoy the occasion. Think of hearing Channing utter his divine enthusiasm in the Pine Woods! It will be, I suppose, in the afternoon, but you shall have farther particulars. Of course you'll come! We can't all be disappointed. Fred brought me a beautiful blue and white violet today, that was new to me. I've been painting

[1] Not Albert Brisbane.

it and other kinds of violets. The flowers come faster than I can paint them. Oh Anna! I have a world of thoughts, and a world of feelings to share with you, and a heart full of happiness to cheer you with — why can't you be here with me in the body, as I know you are in the spirit? Every day adds so much beauty to nature! And this bright youth of the year harmonizes so well with the dawn, the youth of humanity, upon which it is just entering. The great doctrines of Association fire my soul every day more and more. I am awed at the vastness of the schemes it unfolds, I am filled with wonder and ecstacy. I never knew happiness and joy before; and this is not a transient, momentary feeling, but a deep, solemn joy has taken possession of my soul, from the consciousness that there is something worth living for. In the hopes and views that the associative life has disclosed to me, I feel that I have a treasure that nothing can deprive me of. Write soon. We are to have a series of discourses or lectures on Sundays. — Fred says he would like to have you send out that letter, as you must not for a long while attempt to read one. In love

Marianne

Brook Farm, Sunday a.m., May 16, [*1845*].[1]

My dear Anna,

I made a mistake this a.m. (perhaps in consequence of sleeping in Amelia's room), and caught myself up at half-past four, and don't know how to spend the time better than with you. The singing of the birds is really bewildering, — it makes one almost dizzy with the sweetness of harmony.

[1] This letter is incorrectly dated. Since no Sunday in May 1844, 1845, or 1846 fell on the 16th, I have placed it here on internal evidence alone, assuming that it should have been dated May 18.

The sky is cloudy, but I do hope for the girls' sake that the rain will keep off, for never was the garden around us so blooming, so freshly green, and in every way so inviting. It seems wrong to lose a moment of so much beauty and prophecy; — I would be abroad in the midst of it all the time. But alas! indoor duties present their claims. What means this word duty? If duty be not attraction, I don't believe in it. What a state of things the world presents when one cannot do the right, without, at the same time, committing a wrong, — or rather, where the very best thing one can do, cannot be wholly right. Suddenly now the rain is pouring down, — a most beautiful shower! And just as the earth needs it. Oh! this is truly a wonderful season. Our hills and meadows are the richest green. The trees have put forth their blossoms in rare elegance, and profusion, — summer flowers have sprung from the earth in such haste and abundance as to tell of infinite treasures beneath. It seems as tho' the earth were overflowing with hope and promise, so that it can not contain itself, and finds expression in these sweet breathing blossoms. Oh! it is too beautiful! Nature and the animal creation here seem to be in advance of humanity. Nothing speaks to me more eloquently of the repose and the love spirit that shall prevail in Association, than the social state of animals with us. I have spoken to you perhaps of our domestic animals, our cats and dogs, — who go from house to house and are equally at home in either, — a thing I never observed in civilization. A gun is never fired here, — not a child on the place appears to have the least disposition to molest a bird's nest, — and the birds are in consequence surprisingly tame, — they do not fear our steps, they come to us to be fed. Last night, a whippoorwill took shelter in our back room. Mr. Klienstrup and Mr. Allen take much satisfaction in their pet squirrels and quails, which come out of the woods to make them daily visits.

A few days ago, I found the first *trientales*, one with five and another with eight leaves. I put them in W. H. C.'s room. He afterwards told some one he had found two beautiful flowers in his room. Yesterday I went to Cow Island — found wild geranium, ladies' slipper, — solomon's seal — dogwood, trientalis and, what was wholly new to me, — a yellow violet, streaked with purple. This of itself was a treasure. Yesterday also brought to light another wonder — a white pedate violet. I found too the arabis, common about here but new to me. The river, the trees, the wood-paths, all make the walk enchanting, — I should like to take it again with you. I have been painting the trillium.

I love the good Channing more and more. He has felt our reserve here. He cannot, like Mr. Kay, find his way into all our rooms and make acquaintance with us whether we will or not. We must go halfway or more to meet him. He has called on Mrs. Palisse and Mrs. Hosmer (at their invitation), and not elsewhere that I know of. I hope Brattleboro' will restore his health, and that in a very few weeks he will return to us and spend the summer in compliance with our earnest invitation. I think he will be here at the convention.

You have done nobly in the subscription business. I am astonished at your success. Heaven grant we may be faithful, so that great good may grow out of the means thus put into our hands. I don't know now what sum has been given. Mr. Kay has sent a hundred dollars to the school. I am rejoiced, — it will set us up finely. Mr. Ripley is still in New York. John and W. H. C. propose to go tomorrow, but I doubt if John will be well enough. I like your plan of the May festival very much. I made it known to Mrs. Ripley, Orvis, Allen and others, who all approved. — I don't think I shall find any unwillingness here to have it put into execution, if I do, I will say so at the end of this letter. I think a great interest may be got up by that time. Some Lowell people will gladly aid. Mrs. Tarr of Gloucester, a woman of immense energy will lend her helping hand. No doubt it will succeed, if you can only get it started, — if the Roxbury ladies don't say nay. The circular is well drawn up. Last Sunday I went with M. A. Willard and J. O. to the street to hear W. H. C. Today we have him here. . . .

Monday a.m. Had a sweet little walk in the woods before tea with Helen and J. O. We gathered some flowers for you. You must come out, all of you, if we have a June festival, as is probable. Yesterday was a lovely day, — and the rain, tho' it deprived us of a walk to Cow Island, did but make everything more beautiful. Mrs. R. had a note from Mrs. Peabody relative to the plan for next May. — She likes it, but waits for Mr. R. to return previously to sending her answer. I am longing to see you, have much to say. I wish we could keep Helen here awhile, we have so much for her to enjoy. J. O. sends his love to you, and wishes he could see you here. . . .

Yours with love
Marianne

Sunday eve, May 25, [*1845*].

My dear Anna,

Would that you and I understood Phonography — we must learn it, to expedite our correspondence. What say you? Here I have matter for a long talk and must be content to write almost nothing of it. First, your letter was delightful. Being in Mr. and Mrs. Ripley's room, I read them a few lines, and both said good things of you and expressed an earnest desire to have you here. If you could come and board awhile, independently of your father, would you do so? My reason for asking is this. I am in great need of help in painting fans and lampshades, and I believe you do paint some, and might help me. You have painted, have you not? You know, it requires no great skill. Now if you could come at once and help our group some, such help Mrs. Ripley and I think would pay your board. I throw this out for your consideration, catching at every possible chance of getting you here for a few weeks, as a drowning man catches at a straw. Perhaps this could be managed, what think you?

Mrs. Ripley wishes me to ask you, if you should hear of any one who would like a zephyr shawl made and could get an order for one, to let us know. She has made the arrangements for getting them in case we have orders, but don't think it worth while to proceed without. How I hate to write to you on business matters!

The council of science have invited me to be present at all their readings, discussions and business meetings. This will be a great advantage to me, of which I gladly avail myself tho' I can't conceive that I shall be of any use to them, but they will have it so.

The amusement group are preparing for the first of June. I think we shall have a fine time. Monday, if pleasant, is to be the day. Parke Goodwin will not come probably. You and Helen, Mr. and Mrs. Cheney must come Monday afternoon and be here by three o'clock, and you or Helen must be left with us for a week or so. I should say *both* of you, if I knew where to sleep you. Mrs. Ripley says she should esteem it a favor to have Cheney come, but I am almost afraid, in our present crude state, to have him look round here with his artist eye. Ye Gods! what will he think! And yet, it is the true artist who can, better than any other, look thro' the actual and see the beautiful ideal, — the *true* that we have in prospect. Let him come.

Our painting group is bewitching and keeps me constantly excited. Every day gives to my spirit new life and vigor for the work I have to do here. How it unfolds itself constantly more and more, in new beauty and order! Oh! I regret nothing but my littleness, my weakness and inability. Why am I, so insignificant and powerless, lent to this sublimest work, whilst thou, a spirit borrowed from the future age of harmony to show us the way to it, cannot put thy hand to it? But I see it; the coarser, material part should be the machinery, whilst thou art a part of its directing spirit. You cannot tell the good that such as you are doing us, — comfort yourself with that.

Write soon and give love to all, and if you can bring Fanny with you on Monday, do so, — for the children are to have a fete she will enjoy. Newcomb has not returned. Fred was pleased at the correctness of your impressions with regard to that letter. In love

Mary Ann

Send letters for me to Frank, and not to Miss Peabody's. Our fans are elegant — we get a dollar and a dollar and a half apiece.

Friday a.m., June 6, 1845.

Dear Frank,

. . . How shall I tell you of Monday?[1] Such a day does not belong to the calendar, but is one of the eternal

[1] The June festival had taken place on Monday, June 2. Compare Hawthorne's description in the *Blithedale Romance* of a similar occasion.

days. Already it seems far off in antiquity, yet stands out vivid and bright, as one never to be forgotten. And you were not here. I am almost glad it is not in my power to tell you what you lost. Mrs. Parsons came from Hingham, so did the Wilders and their children. As I shall see you so soon, I will not undertake a description, but only say that Channing, Clarke, John, Ripley and others were inspired. Channing and John were beautiful and like angels, and all the people, yes, our common every day people here, were transformed into beautiful beings, — beautiful beyond the sculptor's art. I don't know where this effect came from, but I can recall group after group, worthy of Raphael or Canova. There seemed some enchantment about it, — there were, as John said, child-angels and Madonnas. . . .

Adieu
Marianne

Sunday p.m., [*Summer, 1845*].

Upon my word, dear Anna, this is the best paper I have, and I don't know how I shall get along with it, but my heart is with thee and I must write. . . .

Soon we are to have a lecture from Brisbane in the Pine Woods; will you not come and sit then by my side? I know I shall feel that you are with me. It is a beautiful day, — the face of nature becomes constantly fairer and more beautiful, as the summer advances. What a language does it speak to me! What is the soul, what are its gems and flowers, which all this external loveliness, this varied beauty faintly typifies, but never satisfactorily represents? It seems to me as if a whole volume were written on every leaf, as if every breeze were singing in poetry the deep mysteries of the inner life. Oh! that I were childlike enough, — transparent enough, to receive the lessons so simply and beautifully taught! You, Anna, know more of this than I do, — you, who are a child of heaven, "*a good child.*" Alas! *I* am but a child of earth.

We have noble spirits here at Brook Farm. I have been much affected lately, by the noble devotedness of our good Mrs. Cheswell. This coarse woman, as I once thought her, and as she was, is really becoming very charming, — a most zealous and untiring worker, full of nobleness and enthusiasm in a good cause, sweet and cheerful too, so that it does one good to look upon her. In her, we see what Association is going to do for the uneducated and rude. It *must* call out what is great and noble, what is loving and kind. Friend C. K. N. is kind and sociable. I talk more with him than usual. Yesterday he came into my drawing class — so I appointed him a committee to examine the scholars' books, which office he readily accepted and staid some time and expressed an approbation which was very gratifying to my pride as a teacher, because he was really in earnest. He said considerable about learning to draw himself, — has asked after you with interest.

My life has in it nothing new. Every day I pray for strength to become universal, to care nothing for my own little individual interests, except where they are so real as to be for the interest of humanity also.

Evening. I found, dear Anna, the time had come for the lecture, so had to stop writing. Mr. Brisbane's subject was the organization of a Phalanx — He was interesting, said some excellent things upon the condition of woman, the way she is sold into marriage in civilization. You know

Fourier says it takes 810 individuals to make one perfect or complete man, morally and intellectually, just as it requires both man and woman and 810 muscles — a singular analogy. For a long time it has not seemed correct to me to say that any two persons are *one* being — they may be in harmony, but are far from constituting a complete being.

I do like the Harbinger very much; it ought to be an instrument of much good, may it bring many to the good work. I send you a little sweet briar, and should send more of the mitchela if I had not given it to Newcomb, because he was so delighted with it. I am actually studying Phonography, I wish you would undertake it. We have our lessons at ½ past 5 Sunday morning. You enquired the price of my wild flowers. I don't know. I can't tell yet how many I shall have in the set, but suppose that I might paint them for fifty cents a sheet, — that is little enough for the work. I have engaged to paint a dozen for a lady at that price. Thank you for the book of flowers. It is good, and will be useful to me. When will Mr. Cheney come out again? and Welles — ask him to bring *you* to us. I am glad to learn from John that you heard Ole Bull [1] last evening. — Should like to have been with you. Alas! the poor painting group. Amelia goes to Milton on Thursday to stay a month. Will be in Boston during that time, — sends her love to you and says she will call and see you. I have seen Mary once, she was pleasant, seemed glad to see me. It is queer — well, no matter. What is not clear now will become so in time. . . .

It will not do for me to talk with you longer now with my pen. I must go to the Eyrie and will take you there with

[1] Ole Bull was playing in a second series of concerts in Boston.

me if you will go. I long to see you, — have much to tell and talk about and hear about. Do write very soon.

Yours in love
Marianne

Caroline must read the Harbinger.

Thursday a.m., July [*1845*].

Dear Frank,

. . . Brisbane has given two lectures to his scientific class. They interested me very much but we all want more proof than is forthcoming. The wisest teachers we have are too ignorant for us, and Fourier, if he knew the serial law, has given us not much more than his assertion for it. The Ripleys, Brisbane, Fanny Mac and Dana go to Woburn tomorrow to the workingmen's convention. Will the weather be pleasant, think you? The Macs have cousins here, 2 ladies and a gentleman to stay three weeks (fashionables and enemies of Association). Mr. and Mrs. Monday have come, tailors, and of the better looking sort of people. I miss Amelia. These cousins of Eunice's occupy her room, and our group consequently is scattered, and again, as of old, I paint alone in my room, which is not very agreeable. . . .

Do, if possible, come and be with us tomorrow.

Yours affectionately
Marianne

Brook Farm, August 1, '45.

Dearest Anna,

I received your letter last evening, and you must believe that I am exceedingly grateful for every line I get from you, even if I cannot find a chance to tell you so. These summer months seem our very busiest season — there is no end to the company and no end to the work. When I do write a line, it is so hurried that I forget or omit many things I would tell you. And here let me speak of the pleasant call from Mr. Cheney with his sister, etc. She is a lovely being, and won my admiration at once. Mrs. Ripley walked with us and we really enjoyed the call, which was too short. . . . I have to omit many wild flowers for want of time, or else from head-ache. The field lily I want much, but can't find. I've just been looking over your note, that I may answer it somewhat regularly. Don't be alarmed. I shall not go over a precipice if I know it, and I believe if I follow the promptings of the inner voice, I shall not get into danger. I trust in Heaven, and feel safe, and don't apprehend any change in my life.[1] . . .

The Seeress[2] for some pages pleased me much, but as a whole, I don't much like it. The fact is there are so many stories told in it which I can't believe, that it takes much from the satisfaction I should have in the rest of the book. . . . Channing spent last Sunday with us. — I don't know yet when to expect him again. It was delightful to have him with us, I assure you. Today he was at Waltham. A few of our people were at Dedham. John and Orvis say they had a stupid time. The best speakers were Parker, Garrison and Ryckman. Frank Cabot left home today to go on a whaling voyage before the mast — a sad thing to his family. We have had two arrivals this week — two daughters born to Brook Farm. Mrs. Cheswell's, a fine healthy child,

[1] This is in answer to Miss Parson's warning against becoming too much interested in John Orvis.

[2] Translated by Mrs. Catherine Crowe from the German of Justinus Kerner, 1845. Compare p. 24, n. 5.

— Mrs. Hosmer's apparently strong, healthy and beautiful in form, — but with a fatal disease, affecting its spine and brain, which makes its speedy death desirable and probable. The poor little thing passed the first day of its life here with me in my room. There is no end to our strange experiences in Association. . . .

I wish you could look from my window, and see the corn waving on the hills. My little view was never so beautiful as now, the grounds are under excellent cultivation, and it is really refreshing to the soul to look at them. You see I am too tired and stupid to write, so enough for to-night.

(*Unsigned*)

Brook Farm, August 6, 1845.

Dear Frank,

. . . I send you the notes of "Fourier."[1] The reading satisfied and gratified Brisbane and Channing very much. I think she went deeply into his character and would have gone more into detail, had she had more strength and more time. These notes are very correct, for I took my pencilled ones into the Pine Woods Monday forenoon, and there reviewed and wrote them off with Anna. There may be some expressions which you will not quite understand without a verbal explanation. Anna says she had many impressions impossible to express in language. Of the visible presence of Fourier in the room at the time (and he staid some time) she cannot in language give an idea, — but says it was real, and her communion with him, by question and answer, as real as any communion she has with any living person. I doubt not the truth of this; and the fact disclosed to her of the ineradicable effects of sin, is a very

[1] Anna Parsons's reading of Fourier's character will be found in the Appendix of this book.

interesting and important one to us all, and a confirmation of an opinion I have long held. It is not enough intellectually to *believe* this, we should feel it in our hearts, — and how soon would the individual life and the life of society be regenerated! Of the dark, the horrible, and demoniacal period of Fourier's life alluded to by her, Brisbane says he knows all. It was in the midst of the French Revolution. He plunged into that, — joined the military, and gave himself up recklessly to the vices of the soldiery. Anna steadily refused to analyze this part of his character, altho' Brisbane questioned her much, — but she was firm — feeling that something would be revealed more terrible than her strength could bear. I am glad she resisted. Anna felt rather weaker than usual on Monday, but did not feel the effects of the reading so much as I apprehended. They staid with us until five in the afternoon. . . .

Mr. Kleinstrup's new greenhouse is to be built forthwith, I am told, and hear that Frank Shaw provides the money. This is good, is it not? We learn nothing of the robbers yet, tho' suspicious people have been seen with *their arms done up*. The selectmen have offered $300 and Mr. Hatch[1] $300 more reward. No suspicion or doubt rests upon his story now in the minds of the people. He has got so much better as to walk out, and has made an entirely satisfactory statement to the general council. Mr. Brisbane is going to Batavia in a day or two. — Our haymakers are working very hard now. I think of going out to help rake by and by. I am painting wild flowers today — have succeeded pretty well with the spiræa. Am so sorry I can't get a yellow lily — a field lily.

[1] George Hatch was in charge of the sash and blind business, one of the profitable industries at the Farm.

Evening. . . . This evening we have had an areopagus meeting and voted in Mr. Bane. We have had a long discussion on the 10 hour system, etc., etc. This afternoon Harriette J. and I strolled off towards Cow Island woods, and then off to the haymaking, — reached there just as the *lunch* came to them and had the pleasure of serving them and of helping ourselves to a cup of coffee. I found many wild flowers — some new to me and beautiful. . . .

Your
Marianne

Return the notes of Fourier when you come.

Brook Farm, August 11, [*1845*].

Dearest Anna,

I long to tell you what gratification your excellent letter has afforded others as well as myself. I felt that after you had had time to review your impressions and collect your thoughts you would make some valuable addition to those notes, nor was I deceived. Your letter expressed so much to me, that I read it to William Channing and Newcomb and Brisbane with the notes and afterwards to Miss Russell, Mr. Kay and one or two more. I only wish you knew the pleasure the whole afforded them and had been present at the delightful conversations that grew out of it. To me it was full of interest, and I feel that the impression it made upon me must be for my eternal good. What you say of Fourier is excellent. The more I weigh it the better am I pleased. I can hardly think that if you had been stronger, you would have done much better, or gone more deeply into the character. You might perhaps have been more powerfully moved, more filled and fired with his energy and greatness, — but it seems to me you have penetrated the motives and aim of his life — traced the causes and effects, and what more could you have done? You have not changed much my thought of him. If anything, he is more a wonder to me than ever before, because of that dark period of life, yet I see that even that is consistent. St. Simon, you know, did likewise. Mr. Kay thinks that Jesus must have had such an experience,[1] that he could not become the greatest of saints, unless he had previously been the greatest of sinners; he would like to know what he was about during those unknown years of his life. I think this a suggestion worthy of attention, but don't think I can accept the view. Is it necessary to go through the dark road of sin in order to attain to good? It seems to me that the greatest saint must have been *capable* of becoming the greatest sinner, — but not that he must necessarily have gone into the greatest sins. Did you not say "the *dark lines* make the purity less pure"? Tell me your thoughts of this. How beautiful the landscape you painted in that letter! And now behold it all explained. — An old woman whom Fourier was in the habit of visiting daily for a while, once asked him why he had not married — he answered that once he loved a young woman, but after a two years' absence, found she had married another. This was the light of his life, — the sunny stream of hope and joy that gleamed upon him in the star light of sentiment; and afterwards and thence came that sudden plunge into those awful depths, that the pure soul can hardly look into and not be defiled. How much I have thot of Fourier since the reading, and of his present state! I have not time now to tell you all my thoughts connected with this.

[1] This passage is a sample of the free thinking and free speech at Brook Farm which outsiders found sometimes shocking and sometimes ludicrous.

I am sorry for the impression made upon you, — hope you will be enabled, by some pleasanter intercourse with the spiritual world, to escape its effects. I wish you were not going to read any more at present. I fear it will weaken you physically, and you need every strengthening influence. Do be prudent — do resist when possible.

I rejoice that you soon will see W. H. C. Oh! that I could tell him how plainly and truly he has always spoken to my soul, — what strength and courage and hope and faith he has given me. He is the sunshine, the dew from heaven, the healthful air in which the bud within loves to unfold itself, and feels that it may become a flower fit for paradise. Would that I could keep such influences ever around it. But Heaven be praised for all lights — the lesser as well as the greater.[1]

To speak of another matter, — I am glad you think me in a true and safe position. I feel that I am so, and that I ought not to have felt a doubt which I could not but feel. I don't ask nor care for advice, — knowing well that you can't give any thing definite, and that the fact of your giving it would not enable me to follow it. I keep calm and quiet, and wait the result. As I said to you — I resist because that is in my nature, and I yield when I can't help it, — and I guess the whole is not worth thinking or talking about.[2] Mr. Brisbane went today — what do you think? He calls me "*a problem*" — says he can't understand me — me, who don't care to hide any thing, and have not much either to hide or to manifest. I tell him, every soul is a

[1] Marianne Dwight's tone in speaking of Channing is not different from that of other admirers, both men and women. He seems to have been a radiant presence.

[2] A reference to her feeling for Orvis.

JOHN ORVIS

Who married Marianne Dwight.

problem. He says my nature especially demands sympathy. (I know this well enough.) I tell him, we must learn to stand alone, to be above sympathy if need be, — to grow in goodness without it (that is, *human* sympathy), but to seek it where we shall be sure to find it, — in the ideal, — and in the great Soul that is over all and through all, and ever ready to respond to our beating hearts.

Wed. a.m. Good morning, dear Anna, how are you today and how did you spend last evening, which here was wondrously beautiful with mist and moonlight? I will tell you, that quite unexpectedly to both of us, I had a pleasant walk and talk, and pleasant too in that balmy air, with our friend of "*the veil*."[1] Don't speak of villany in connection with Mr. Hatch. There is not room for a shadow of doubt, if one only knew, as we know, the whole of the strange story. I confess to you, it excites my indignation and almost makes me angry to hear doubts, — they have all been dispelled here, since he became able to make a full and clear statement. He has had a relapse, perhaps from over-exertion, and lies now upon his bed, ill and sad and beautiful in suffering. Has raised considerable blood, probably from internal injury — he suffers from his side and head. He has, you know, a sad fault, — but is a man of undoubted honesty here; besides, could have had no motive for all this. Oh, Anna! Brook Farm, I feel, is to you a beautiful dream. You would not realize here all that you hope and believe. It is far better than civilization, it is true; still it is the ideal which animates us to labor that makes life here so full of interest. We have hope and love and faith, shedding down upon us their sweet, inspiring light from a higher world, and

[1] John Orvis. "The veil" is an expression for either his reserve or Miss Dwight's.

perhaps gliding into our hearts more than ever before. . . .

Adieu. A bright and beautiful day to you.

Marianne

Brook Farm. — The last day of summer.
[*Aug. 31, 1845.*]

Dearest Anna,

Your very welcome letter came to me last eve, and if it is not foolish I should like to impart to you some of the feelings which it excited in me. I felt happy and grateful that you, who have such gifted friends, you who have delightful letters from brother angels, could willingly and heartily write to your unworthy Marianne a long letter. I was almost surprised. I was saddened, for I said to myself, — what can I be to thee? — I who am nothing, who am but an aspiration to say the best. And I ask thee, how is it that thou art pleased with such letters as I send thee? Does thy imagination see in the words more than I intend? What dost thou find? It cannot be for aught I say in the letters. Is it then because I have a place in thy heart? Ah! how little a thing am I to dwell in a heart so large. I am almost afraid thou wilt wake up some day as from a dream, and find that nothing is nothing and lose sight of me forever. Forgive my troubling you with such feelings. . . .

C. P. Cranch is with us now. — Last evening he made for us the sweetest and most delightful music. Will anything recall the past so vividly as music? I was carried back to our old home in Boston by hearing the same songs sung by the same sweet, rich voice. The effect was strange. All late events, all this life in Association, its aims, its efforts, its surroundings, seemed to me like a dream, from which I had just awakened.

Oh! Anna, you ask what is there worth doing? . . . I have often the same thoughts and feelings. — But this I believe is certain; we trouble ourselves a great deal too much about what we shall do, — we are not content to remain in our own spheres, and receive the sunshine and the dew that heaven sends us, — but must break violently out of them and go hunting about where we do not belong, and stumbling in paths where our feet can never walk. It is not so difficult a matter to tell what to do. I must do the very thing that lies clearly before me to do this very minute; and that done, — the next minute will bring its own plain work. If I can see into the past and future and understand the universal bearing of each action, why!, so much the more interesting; but this is not necessary to keep me in the right path.

Fear not, — our friend [1] shall not have the honor of preventing me from writing to you. You are marching ahead with your conclusions; you speak of a crisis of which I do not think — or if such a thought comes, I banish it. It is not a matter of thought with me, — something deeper than thought controls here, — but I have nothing new to say — when I see you we will talk. You careless child, to write as you did, and send your letter unfastened by the wafer, — don't do so again.

Last evening ten people came to spend Sunday and we have bestowed them all. You will see Mr. Kay next Sunday if you come. How delightful to hear Mary Bullard sing at our Sunday meeting. . . .

"A new day," yes, that was well said. Channing gave us a pictorial sermon, a sketch of a temple of worship to be raised here on Brook Farm, as he saw it in his mind's eye.

[1] John Orvis.

The picture was real to us, so glowingly was it described. It was sacred and exquisitely beautiful. I never saw anything like it; and there stands that holy temple, I see it yet, of circular form, lighted from above, with its pictures of the infant Jesus, of the crucifixion, and the resurrection — with its white marble altar; that temple where music would rise to heaven and where there would always be flowers. He closed with solemn exhortations to us, to be true, to be earnest, to be wise, etc., etc. It was a comfort to me to feel that he did but repeat to me and renew in me resolutions I had already taken. Would I could be faithful to them!

I miss Mary Lincoln much. The strange child! No one can accuse her of being a civilizee, for she is one of the least civilized beings I have ever met with. I can't help liking her, I believe her aims are high, — but perhaps she is so independent as not to consult sufficiently other people's happiness and convenience — she is very childish — a mere baby in some of her ways; and to this I now attribute many of her odd actions. With much purity, she has, it seems to me, very little delicacy for a woman.

Gossip talks loud at Brook Farm about Charles Dana and Eunice, says they will be united in marriage — perhaps it is not true, — but I do know the symptoms are very strong.

I expect Cranch to paint and draw some whilst here. Mr. Grant is here from the Ohio Phalanx. A Miss Blackwell is with us from Flushing. Mrs. Cote has come back here to board. Sarah W[hitehouse] has gone to New York on a visit. Maria Dana has returned from New Hampshire, is much out of health apparently — I am somewhat anxious about her. . . . Write to me. Give my love to Hingham friends. . . . Adieu, dear friend.

Thy Marianne.

[*September, 1845*].

Dearest Anna,

C. P. C.[1] leaves us today. I cannot help writing a few lines to you. I long to tell how I have enjoyed his visit. I have come nearer to him than ever before. He has sat at the table and painted with me every day that he has been here. Has painted landscapes for our group and one or two for my own unworthy, grateful and happy self. He has sung to us, fluted to us, and mimicked for us all manners of insects and animals. We have made him almost promise to return on Sunday, holding out to him as inducements, the presence of Channing, yourself, Helen, and Mary Bullard. So now once more, I urge you to come, and by all means make Dora come, to whom give much love. I heard of her saying she should back out (don't tell her) if certain noisy girls, Eliza Hersey, etc. (I've not heard the names), should get up an expedition for Brook Farm, as they talked of doing. Between you and me, Anna, wouldn't it do just gently to hint to said pleasure-party, said *spree*-seeking, merry-making girls, that some other occasion might be pleasanter both for them and for us? — and more convenient too, — for we shall have many people here. Pray, don't mistake me. I know you feel as I do, that we don't want our Sabbath, our high and highest holy day intruded on, or broken in upon by those who are of other spirit and seek for different enjoyments than we look forward to on that occasion, — and why not let them know it? I am ever glad to see them at the right time. If your first proposed party don't come, it will disappoint us more than I can tell. Don't let anything prevent. How much I want to see you all, and you especially.

(*Unsigned*)

[1] Cranch.

Brook Farm, Sunday, Sept. 28th, [*1845*].

My dear Anna,

I will talk to the girls and write to you at the same time. . . . And now what shall I select from the great heap I have to tell you? Last evening we had a party to express our kind feelings to Mr. Ryckman previously to his leaving for the winter, a *very* pleasant party, — many fine things said. Wish you could have heard John (D.) when he said, "*Channing is ours*," and such thunders of approbation followed. Thy brother [1] felt too much for words, and spoke but few in reply, and those few so wise, so modest, so full of meaning!

Evening. The girls are gone — you see I did not accomplish my letter, — and now for another attempt. How much we have enjoyed their visit! They are spending the evening, or a part of it, at "Ma Cabot's" with Fred, Mary and J. Orvis. And so you are sorry you was "treacherous," are you? Well, to punish you, I guess I won't tell you any more. And yet, I will tell you this, that friends never spoke more openly or confidingly to each other.[2] It is delightful to have so true an intercourse with anyone, — to speak so unreservedly. And now I think I have written enough on this subject, — how can I write? You would hardly believe such strange things as I might say. There is *no veil* in *my* presence now, thank Heaven, for that! Oh! what dear, what blessed friends Heaven sends me. Do, dearest Anna, speak a word to me to enable me to feel and bear the gratitude I ought, and how shall I, in return, bless these loving hearts?

We have had lately a shaking up, as it were, a little sifting out. Some deep and important questions have been agi-

[1] *I.e.* Channing. [2] A reference to a conversation with John Orvis.

tated. Some will leave who ought to leave. The selfish should go — they who are not devoted, who cannot give their all. It is a question, how much ought one to give. I must retain *this* at least. I must be master over myself, and be sure that I am working for my own idea and not blindly following wherever I may be led. Do you think your father will let you come and board here awhile? Have you asked him, or shall you ask? We have had a delightful visit from Mr. Kay; such nice little chats, — and such delightful times late in the evening when a few of us would be gathered in his room to eat crackers and cheese. He is the most delightfully entertaining man. Lizzie Curson is perfectly charming. I have no words to tell you how beautifully, how wisely and lovingly and harmoniously she moves about here in every sphere. Oh! that we had a dozen such girls, or would that we had even this one — alas! her visit will very soon be over. She speaks in highest terms of your friend and her friend, Lucy Hudson, knows she would be very useful here, etc., etc. The girls will tell you so much that you can the better excuse me for saying no more now, — for the fact that I write with some difficulty is proof enough to me that I am sleepy and ought to be in bed. . . .

And now, dear, good night.

Your loving friend
Marianne

Thanks for the beautiful gentians.

Sunday p.m., Oct. 5, 1845.

My dear Anna,

I will send you now a few more grains from "the heap," and you must take them as they come. W. H. Channing and Mr. Brisbane both are here, so is Mr. Grant. I suppose you will not have a yearning for the Eyrie parlor at about four o'clock! W. H. C. came in one of his brightest moods last evening, and Lizzie says he preached gloriously at the street this a.m. But I am going to leave off picking up the grains this minute and turn aside. . . .

I have now a plan, which I will begin to execute tomorrow, of making some little books for sale. I hope that in your zeal for Association, you will not buy up at once the whole edition! They are to be picture books — wild flowers, birds, and I know not yet what variety. I want to have them as low-priced as possible, — perhaps some for fifty cents, some seventy-five or a dollar. The only question is whether I can do them so, with any profit to ourselves — perhaps half a dozen or a dozen pictures in a book. Can you make any suggestion? I intend to have the cover of colored Bristol-board, prettily stamped, like our fans and shades. What think you, will they not sell for presents, especially at Christmas and New Year? Would you have a beautiful verse of poetry attached to each picture, provided it could be just the thing? . . .

Evening. We have had our meeting — a conversational one, considering what shall be our meetings, our worship, our church.[1] Many suggestions were made. W. H. C. dreads giving the lead to the priesthood, thinks the prophets (they who are inspired with deep, true feeling) must lead. He wants a place consecrated to worship. We talked of taking for the purpose a large room in the Phalanstery, which can be ready soon. Some want worship every morn-

[1] From this time on, the reader observes something like a religious revival taking place at the Farm under the influence of Channing. The movement was apparently distasteful to some of the members. See post p. 124. So far as I can discover, this new element in the life has not been taken into account in discussing the history of Brook Farm.

ing, — some want conversation open to all, — some want music, — or rather *all* want it, — prayer, too, — silent worship, — instruction. All these are good, — but no plan, no form of worship that is practicable can meet my wants, or perhaps anyone's. Next Sunday we propose to form a group of all interested and choose a [chief] to see about getting the room, and making all arrangements. To-day, for the first time, came to me a satisfactory idea of a true form of worship. Of course, the whole of life should be worship — all labor, consecration, and not desecration, — and so all life should be poetry, should be music. But as we have a particular expression of poetry and of music, but adapted to these sentiments, why may we not have a form of worship peculiarly adapted to the religious sentiment? And now let me try to unfold my idea, tho' I can't do it justice. I think we must have in perfect Association, worshipping series, — comprising various groups. I may go to the temple filled with the spirit of prayer, and you at the same time may want song and thanksgiving, — another may want silent worship, another preaching. Now I see a most beautiful temple, spacious and elegant, divided into various apartments, or temples, or *sanctums*. Here is one for the group of prayer, one for music, one for silent social worship, rooms for solitary devotion, — a large central hall, where all may gather when inspired with a universal sentiment, — the hall of unity, — and there give utterance to it. This is a very imperfect sketch of a picture which to me has great beauty in it. I am getting to love it — believe there is truth in it. I have mentioned it to Mrs. Ripley and one or two more who like it much. How does it affect you? Oh the heap — the heap! Every grain I take away raises the pile higher — so, in mercy to you and to Frank who waits for me at the Eyrie, I must stop. . . .

Love to all
Marianne

Pilgrim House, Sunday a.m., Oct. 19, '45.

My dear Anna,

A bright, beautiful Sabbath morning, and *you* in Boston! . . . All the week I have wished to write to you to tell you of last Sunday. It was the busiest day! In the morning, almost everything to do, — in the afternoon a walk to Oak Hill, — then our Eyrie meeting. Channing gave us a very fine address, speaking of the three aspects of Association, the economical, the social, the *religious*, dwelling especially upon the last; he expressed his deep conviction that without the religious element no attempt at Association could possibly succeed, and then he spoke particularly, with much warmth and enthusiasm, much beauty and eloquence, of the religious movement now taking place here. Finally, alluding to the presence of a good many strangers, and of some other persons who take no interest at all in the matter, he proposed that all who felt themselves prepared or in any way interested in the movement, should withdraw to the next room, to take measures for carrying it into execution. About twenty went into the library. I was perplexed, astonished, I expected a full rush of people, — I asked if I were doing right, if we all had done right, to come out of the room. But I saw no way to avoid it. We could not have done otherwise, — it was a necessary step in order to form any organization; with W. H. C. and others I felt sure it grew out of the deepest feeling, and I was with them, because I did not feel that I could be left out. Some who were known to be deeply interested stayed behind and this was not pleasant. Channing spoke to us on the subject for which we were met, went over the whole ground, expressed the widest and broadest spirit, the most earnest desire to have the full cooperation of all. We all joined hands and united in prayer that we might be earnest and devoted and true to each other, and declared that the presence of anyone in our devotions should entitle one to be one of our band. We want no other exclusiveness than this — to protect ourselves, if we can, against the presence of those who would come only to scoff and ridicule. The mere presence of such people is enough to chill devotion, or any social feeling. We appointed a committee of seven to make the arrangements for worship, Mr. Channing, Mr. Dwight, Mr. Shaw, Mr. Monday, Mrs. Ripley, Fanny Mac and M. A. Dwight. This committee met directly after tea, — appointed W. H. C. and Frank Shaw to wait on Mr. Rogers, and arrange with him to have a large room at this end of the Phalanstery, in the second story, finished off immediately (by Christmas) as a consecrated place of worship for the time being, to be used for no other purpose. We wish to make this as beautiful as possible with our means, and as appropriate. We expect to raise money by subscription. Mr. Channing proposed to take it upon himself to send out during the week such books as we would want, — Mr. Clarke's and the Swedenborgian ritual or book of worship. We thought the service must commence with music. At the first service we desire to have only our group (I don't use the word technically) present, — that is, only the *interested*, — the sincere worshippers. Then we may have reading of the scriptures — we may have prayer — silent devotion, with an opportunity for any to speak who may be deeply moved. The exercises will be left to the person who may conduct them for the day. Mr. C. will not be considered as a priest — we do not want a priest. These services are to be closed with music, during which the doors will be open to all who may choose to come to hear an address from some one. This is an imperfect sketch of our present plan. Most carefully will we guard against sectarianism, against dead forms. After the committee meeting was over we joined a social party of all, in the Eyrie parlor, which is to take place every Monday evening. At half past nine a few friends came over to the Pilgrim [House] to help us despatch sweet potatoes. Had a merry time, especially as the Archon and George Curtis were with us, and as we met on the way an invitation to a coffee party from Mr. Brisbane at ten. There we stayed till past twelve — W. H. C., J. O., J. S. D.[1], etc., etc., talked much and were quite interesting. It seemed many people didn't like the withdrawal from the Eyrie parlor in the afternoon. Among them Mary Lincoln and J. Orvis. There was some misunderstanding. I am writing a short, unpoetical, matter-of-fact letter, because of the immense heap of such facts. W. H. C. was most beautiful, most hearty, most loving. I felt that Heaven was with us, by bringing him among us. He says he is going to write to you to give up that other life (the letter reading), both for the sake of your health and your character. He thinks with me that is not good to be put into other people's sphere in that way. Has he written?

Last evening we had a dance. — W. H. C. dances with much grace and vivacity. Our Fanny was so happy as to have him for a partner. Mr. Kleinstrup is acquainted with

[1] Channing, Orvis, and Dwight.

that flower, — says it is of the amaranth kind. It has not *beauty* enough to recommend itself to him. For a few days I have been living a sweet life among the violets. We have, in the greenhouse, the finest collection I have ever seen, and I have tried to transfer some of them to paper. As I paint, I acquire a real passion for them. The violet has become a new flower to me, and speaks to me the most cheering and sympathetic and loving language.

Sunday evening. We have had a delightful day. Our meeting was full of interest. Many more joined us. I thought I never had felt my heart so expand with love, — I never had experienced anything so like *social* worship before. Messrs. Ripley, Wolcott, Allen, Orvis and Kleinstrup were added to our committee. Channing directed his remarks to us to three points. First, that we should avoid rallying around a priest, but should feel that the spirit of Love was the centre of union — that God was with us. 2d, that we should not unite in a creed (for the truth is not yet revealed) but in the spirit of reverence for truth, and in patience waiting for it to come. 3d, that we must exercise charity, — for every resolution we break we must have a new vow, for every fault in another, a new forgiveness.

Your note is yet unanswered. With regard to Mary B.'s coming — First, tell her she *must* come, if she *can* and has any Christian love for us. What should we think of *you* if you *could* come and *didn't?* On what terms she can come I can't tell exactly, but will make such enquiries as will perhaps enable me to answer your questions. I think four dollars the usual rate per week for board, washing, etc., where no work is done. Can you tell me on what conditions she would like to come? And if you can, will you? — I suppose she would prefer to work some, would she not, — and how much? I may possibly be in town on Thursday. If so, I will see you. Am sorry Mary and Helen did not come today. My eyes are too weak for me to write now — so fare thee well.

In much love
Marianne

Sunday eve., Nov. 9, '45.

My dear Anna,

Thanks for your letter. Here are Fanny and I, shut up in our room. Fanny sends her love, and wishes you were in quarantine with us. Such times and such *humbugry* even here in Association! I don't know that anybody has had the small pox yet but little Fred Allen [1] (and his case was slight), but as a precautionary measure the Cottage has been turned inside out, (and our elastic Pilgrim House has swallowed up its contents) and has been made into a hospital, and thither Fred [2] has been carried with his attendants, and Fred's father — who has either slight vareoloid or a cold — I don't know which, and Osborne [3] is imprisoned there as his nurse, and two men, symptomatic people, have been added to the number. Fanny [4] has had for three days one of her old colds, and day before yesterday was quite sick, — today is quite well, only a little headache and weak, and Amelia and Fanny Mac have made a muster, and frightened the folks into thinking it vareoloid. It's the greatest absurdity in the world. So this morning the Archon urged her going to the Cottage. I told him, no —

[1] John Allen did not believe in vaccination. His motherless small boy had the first case of smallpox. There was a serious epidemic but no fatal case.

[2] Fred Allen. [3] Osborne Macdaniel. [4] Fanny Dwight.

that I would not yield my common sense to other people's absurdities. He said Fanny Mac gave it as her opinion that Fanny had the disease and Amelia was much alarmed. I said Fanny Mac knew nothing about, and I didn't value her opinion in the matter, the least in the world, and we, knowing very well just Fanny's condition, would not risk sending her where she would be in danger of taking the contagion, unless some physician whose opinion I could respect said she had the symptoms. I told him it was ridiculous, nonsensical, and unreasonable, and that it was no easy matter for me to yield my sense of right to such follies; that if she had the symptoms she would thankfully go, but I would not trust that to any of the girls, for I tho't they were very ignorant in such matters. Finally he tho't she'd better not go to the Cottage, but I must seclude myself as well as her, and stay in our room all day and see what tomorrow would bring forth. I, of course, expressed that this was equally ridiculous and absurd, told him that to allay the panic of the people I would stay up for meals and not go among folks. So I have not seen our glorious Channing. I believe I am a *consummate fool* to have lost this. Oh! I said worse and harder things still to Mr. Ripley, for I knew that the panic, in Fanny's case, was a *got up* fear, and not a natural one. We've had a pretty good day of it. Some folks would come in, in spite of the quarantine, and then I've been to walk in the Phalanstery corridor. I've sewed and read. Fanny is nicely, and it seems to us such a farce, such a sham, that we make ourselves quite merry about it. I don't apprehend that the disease will spread here, to any extent. Many people have colds. Father has quite a severe cold. I don't know but the Cottage may get populous with people so afflicted. . . .

I've really raved today, — getting quite mad (John Cheever like) because the other people have gone mad. I'm sure I forgive them with all my heart, am just as friendly as ever, and check, as much as I can, every childish pang at the unfriendliness of some who are dear to me. . . .

It has been too wet to go into the woods, or I should send you "a sprig." Can you wait? Martin has just come in, and we're having a nice time. He says Mary Bullard is coming after Thanksgiving — this is good news. Oh! Anna, I don't like to give up your coming — still I hope — and so must thou. Dear, dear friend, I long for thee. I am glad you were pleased with the flowers. Don't regret the time they took me. It was a very little while, and could not have been better spent. They talk too much for me to write. Give my love to all. Write soon. When the panic is over, Fanny and I may go in for a day. I'm glad you are having the pleasure of learning German. Oh! keep up your heart, the winter will bring its riches to you, and you will continually impart to me and others your own riches.

Adieu — in love to thee —
Marianne

Lucy Hudson's plants came, and Mr. K.[1] likes them much.

Monday evening, Nov. 10, [*1845*].

Dear Frank,

I keep my promise and send you a bulletin of health. Father is perhaps some better. — I guess he will be pretty well tomorrow, — tho' he has not been so well as he appeared in the morning. Has kept his bed nearly all day. Mother is much better, needs rest. Fanny is quite well —

[1] Kleinstrup.

has not been out on account of the high wind. Has a little cold sore upon her lip, which alarmed Eunice, who called me out to ask if I was *sure* she had not eruption. I told her I would not listen to any such nonsense, and afterwards told her from Fanny, that Fanny was perfectly willing to compare faces with her. I went down to dinner. Mr. and Mrs. Ripley looked in consternation, but not a word has been said to me. She had previously told Martin he must not come to our room, and forthwith he came. I found nobody else alarmed to see me but all rather glad. And now comes the richest. When in the kitchen this evening, I heard Amelia was sick. Someone says, "Is she going to the Cottage?" "Oh yes, if she is not better tomorrow, she *wishes* to." "Yes," says Maria Dana seeing me, "Miss Russell has *too much sense*, not to respect people's feelings about it." I could not help saying, "I hope she has sense enough to *know* whether she has the vareoloid or not."

After coming home, Maria went in to see Miss Russell. I sent word to her that if she was ill I would gladly go and see her, and do anything for her I could, provided she was not afraid of me. She sent word she was not, so I went to her. In came Eunice, "Why Miss R. are *you* sick?" "Yes, I'm sick." "You don't think it possible you could have the vareoloid?" "Oh la! no indeed, I've a bad cold, and have a sick head-ache — shall be well enough in the morning." Rather rich, was it not? Just what she would not allow to be true of Fanny.

Mrs. Palisse has been on her bed all day. Dr. Stimpson says it's nothing but a cold. Mr. Blake has a cold, — Kate Sloan has symptoms, etc., etc. When I entered the kitchen at noon, Ma Ripley called out very cheerfully, "Hallo, here comes Mary Ann!" "Yes," said I, "Mary Ann is quite tired of the sham." Nobody feared me, or has feared Fanny, except Amelia, Mrs. R. and Fanny Mac.

It's a brilliant evening, *perfectly glorious*. I wish you were here. I've had a fine day's leisure, for I couldn't go into Amelia's room to get my painting materials. Many people are beginning to laugh at the panic. I hope you didn't take cold going in. Mr. Dana goes in tomorrow. I do hope *I* shall not get a cold. I will write you again by the next opportunity, to tell you how father and mother get along.

Your affectionate sister
Marianne

All well this a.m. — *Tuesday*.

Tuesday evening, Nov. [*11*,] *1845*.

Dear Frank,

Have just received your *pleasant* note and now for a little more fun, tho' I am heartily sick of the nonsense, and trust it has now come to an end. This morning as I was waiting on table Mr. Ripley called me to him, and requested that I would not endanger people as I did; it was not safe for one who had been so exposed to come down to the dining-room. I asked him how *exposed?* "Why, you've been much with Fanny." "Well," said I, "*she* hasn't been exposed, more than all of us, and has had no contagious disease, and is coming out herself today." Said he, "It is tho't she has the disease." "Who thinks so?" said I. "Many people have seen her, and no reasonable person thinks she has had anything but a cold." "Why," said he, "there's Miss Mac thinks so." (Fanny Mac and Mrs. R. heard all.) Said I, "I told you, the other day, what I tho't of Miss M.'s opinion. I violated my sense of right and duty by staying away Sunday, and I can on no account consent to act so again. I will use no more needless caution." He requested me not to wait on Mr. Hatch, nor on *his* table, and not to come into the dining-room. I told him it was of no use, I was convinced what I ought to do, and I should do it. He urged very pleasantly all the while, till I told him I'd say no more, I would not waste words with him and walked off. I also told him it was a got up panic, and confined to three or four. Afterwards he came to me again — begged we would be careful and not appear about. I told him Fanny was as well as he. Said he, "You never can tell till the last minute, she may break out yet." I replied, "She is to all appearance, as well as you now. I don't know what she may have by and by, or what you may have. You may break out. Why don't you go and shut yourself up?" — at which he went off laughing. Fanny went to the Eyrie and spent the forenoon. We *all* went down to dinner and to tea, and have heard no more, except that tonight Fanny Mac made an apology to Frances for having made a statement that had given her friends a false impression of her sickness. I think she is well aware of her error. Amelia is still quite ill, tho' better, — much as Fanny was. Dr. Stimpson says it's nothing but a cold — wonder what she thinks of Fanny now! Abby Foord has come home and would stay in spite of her aunt's wishes — says nobody else is half so much afraid as Amelia. The Cottage has two new inmates, Mr. Capen and George Lloyd. The latter I fear is quite ill.

Wed. evening. What strange experiences we go thro' here! The Cottage is filling up. Mr. Monday, the tailor, Cate Sloan, and Mrs. Palisse have gone there today — all plain cases of vareoloid, so say both father and Dr. Stimpson. Maria Dana has been very ill all the afternoon, is now in Amelia's room for the night. She has the symptoms beyond a doubt, and I fear will be severely ill. I've been with her, and with Mrs. Palisse and have sat at table with Mr. Capen. I could not find it in my heart to neglect the sick people in our own house. Amelia is a little better tonight. Hers don't appear to be vareoloid.

Thursday a.m. I will add that Fanny continues very well and is strong as usual and at work. Mother has resumed her duties. Father seems feeble but is about, and has visited all the sick. There never was such a time here — so many people ill. In the pecuniary way, it must be a great loss to us. It is well we find ludicrous things to laugh at, for there is really a dark side to the affair. Still I trust this is the worst of it, and soon all will be better. Write soon.

In haste
Marianne

Sunday, Nov. 23, 1845.

My dear Anna,

I must have the comfort of saying a few words to you today, — a few of the many you would hear if you were sitting here cozily with me in my room. The state of things here is strange, and in some of its aspects, deeply sad, — yet a general cheerfulness prevails, and I am only astonished that, all things considered, we get along so nicely as we do.[1] The hospital has rendered us back the greater number of its tenants, and except Mrs. Palisse, all are getting well rapidly, and we have no anxiety for any one. But we feel

[1] Miss Dwight was correct in her assumption that none of her own family had or would have the disease.

that this is no small exception. She is a woman so much beloved and exceedingly useful to us! I cannot but feel that she will be restored to us, tho' for several days she has been in a very critical state; the accounts from her continue favorable, but the danger is not over. Her husband and son are with her. She is so changed, people who see her say you would not know her to be a human being. James Ryckman also was perhaps equally disfigured for a while, but not so ill, and is now pretty well. George Lloyd has walked out — may yet live, for aught I see, to fill "Mrs. ——'s pitchers"! These three have been our sickest people, we have had twenty in the Cottage at one time. Had we known, a few weeks ago, that this disease would attack so many of us, I believe we should not have tho't it possible that we could go thro' with it. Heaven only knows now what the result will be. This I know, that my heart is full of thankfulness, of faith, and yet of anxiety. We have fallen upon the critical time. Our Phalanstery will, I suppose (no part of it) be done this season, — there is fresh difficulty with Rogers.[1] How we need capital! If we could get clear of him, and get it all into our own hands, I would not care much then if it all blew away. It wouldn't be by that ill wind that blows nobody any good. If we get along thro' the sickness and other difficulties, as I suppose we shall, we shall soon have as good or a better set of people here than we have ever had. The Treadwells are all ready to come back, Lizzie Curson is coming in three or four weeks to live here. Mary Anne Willard ere many weeks, and I hope we shall have Dora for two months. Oh! how much we are in need of help no one can tell. I don't see how any woman here could, unless from absolute neces-

[1] The contractor in charge of building the Phalanstery.

sity, be thoughtless enough to absent herself a single day. Mrs. Kleinstrup (in spite of her husband's and other people's remonstrances) went off, a day or two ago, to make a long visit, and Mary Lincoln has gone and probably will not return all winter. She took French leave as it were, went over to the street to spend the day. It is not generally known that her plan is to be away all winter, I learned it accidentally. Perhaps if Fred don't go to Philadelphia, she will change her mind. Poor Fred! I believe he feels ashamed to tell anything about it. She is now in Brattleboro' with Mrs. John Brown, who is quite ill.

Eunice is flourishing mightily — is getting to be almost omnipotent, being in the good graces of Charles, — managing the dormitory, the distributing committee, and I know not what. I wish you could see her fly from house to house, from morning till late at eve; you would not think it could take her an hour to put a girdle round about the earth. Maria is out of the hospital and lives at the Eyrie for the time being and so does Osborne, and they are inseparable. What will come from an engagement here, I can't tell; for he is exceedingly unpopular and could not by any possibility, I think, get admitted into the Association. I like him in his place. He is capable and kind; but he is not the man for us now nor the man for Maria.[1]

Would you know my surroundings? Alfred Perkins has the little room next to ours, and John Cheever the one on the other side of us. John O. has gone up into our attic. We have planned some evening readings and expect to have good, pleasant times in this way. I've a great mind to give you a peep under a certain veil, but upon reflection, I will

[1] Osborne Macdaniel's marriage with Maria Dana was apparently a happy one.

not. You must wait. And yet I don't want to be tantalizing, but what I would say I can't very well put on paper, — so I'll leave you to imagine the progress of events. I wish I were worthy of the love and affection that some dear friends lavish upon me.[1] I am sorry to hear that W. H. C.[2] is ill with a slow fever. He has undertaken too much lately, — I do hope he will be more careful in future. He did not come out here last Sunday, on account of the sickness here, and the fears of his friends. How long it seems since I have seen him!

I have no fear or thought of taking the disease, believing myself to be well guarded against it. I helped take care of Mrs. Palisse and Maria before their removal to the Cottage, and also of Alfred Perkins. Now we have no new cases, and I trust we shall hear of no more, — yet it is very possible. It seems the Whitehouses carried this curse with them to the North American Phalanx.[3] Amanda has been ill, ten or eleven days, and Sarah, it is feared, has it, as she had been ill, when we heard, two days. If they did not carry Amanda off the place immediately, — it seems to me unpardonable. Osborne wrote instantly to Sarah, to recommend a general vaccination, a precautionary measure we ought to have taken. Our carelessness has been very blamable. When I get time, I shall go to Boston. Don't know when that will be. What singular weather we are having! The mild weather, prolonged thus into autumn has been a great blessing to us. . . .

Marianne

[1] We may infer that Orvis has proposed and been accepted.

[2] Channing.

[3] At Red Bank, New Jersey.

Brook Farm, Sunday, Dec. 7, 1845.

My dear Anna,

I was glad to get even a few lines from you to day, and feel prompted to say a great many things to you, — but I do not like to put upon paper what I could say to you upon those subjects now of the deepest moment to me. So I will begin at least with more trifling matters — as this — I think I have about recovered my health, — I was obliged to keep shut up a few days, not because I was really ill, but because I was tormented with the itching and burning of an eruption very similar to erisipelas (I *can't* spell it) or St. Anthony's fire. Now I am quite well except a slight cold. We have had no new cases of small pox for two or three weeks, and have no reason to suppose we shall have any more. Our patients have nearly all left the hospital. They are all quite well excepting Mrs. Palisse, who is recovering fast. She came as near death as possible, and it will be long ere she is quite well. She will be, they say, badly marked. Jenny and little Fred will bear the marks a long time, but I thank Heaven it is no worse. I trust the Cottage will soon be restored to us, then the Hosmers will come back and the Treadwells, and soon Lizzie Curson. You speak of a crisis,[1] — this is one of the things I can't write fully about, and whatever I may say will be confidential. We have reached, I believe, our severest crisis. If we survive it, we shall probably go on safely and not be obliged to struggle thro' another. I think here lies the difficulty, — we have not had business men to conduct our affairs — we have had *no* strictly business transactions from the beginning, and those among us who have some business talents, see this error, and feel that we cannot go on as we have

[1] In the financial affairs of the Farm.

done. They are ready to give up if matters cannot be otherwise managed, for they have no hope of success here under the past and present government. All important matters have been done up in council of one or two or three individuals, and everybody else kept in the dark (perhaps I exaggerate somewhat) and now it must be so no longer; — our young men have started "enquiry meetings," and it must be a sad state of things that calls for such measures. We are perplexed by debts, by want of capital to carry on any business to advantage, — by want of our Phalanstery or the means to finish it. From want of wisdom we have failed to profit by some advantages we have had. And then Brisbane is vague and unsteady; the help he promised us from his efforts comes not — but on the contrary, he and other friends to the cause in New York, instead of trying to concentrate all efforts upon Brook Farm as they promised, have wandered off, — have taken up a vast plan of getting $100,000 and starting anew, so they are for disposing of us in the shortest manner, — would set their foot upon us, as it were, and divert what capital might come to us. What then remains for us, and where are our hopes? I will tell you. We must be independent of the New York friends, and define our position to them, and let them know that we are determined to go on, if we can, and come to *something* (what Heaven wills), if we do not realize a perfect association. Then we must raise some money, — we must have $10,000 at least, before spring, or we may as well die! We can do nothing without it. How shall we get it? We will send out our group of lecturers, — John Allen will go; John Orvis will go, provided the council will take such steps first, that he can in conscience ask people to come here, and put in their money. He would not do it without some change of policy, nor would he, I think, be willing to remain. Fred (don't speak of it) has decided, unless he should see reason to change his mind, to leave and go into business awhile. His views and plans are noble, — he means to be working for Association abroad, outside, — and come in, by and by, when he sees a change and bring his earnings. But between you and me, not much would I give for what he will do for Association, if he leaves us — tho' I don't doubt his present intentions. But I look back a year and see what changes have gradually come over his mind, and what influences have been at work upon him, and bro't him to his present convictions, — that Brook Farm cannot succeed. My hopes are here; our council seems to be awake and ready for action; if we get the money, we will finish the building, — then we will enlarge our school, which should bring us in a handsome income. Our sash and blind business is very profitable, and may be greatly enlarged in the spring, the tailor's business is good, the tin block, and why do I forget the printing, and the Farm? Also we shall have together a better set of people than ever before. Heaven help us, and make us wise, for the failure of Brook Farm must defer the cause a long time. This place as it is (take it all in all) is the best place under the sky; why can't people see this, and look upon it hopefully and encouragingly?

J. O. sits with me quietly, reading the President's message. Oh! he is so much more constant and affectionate in his regard for me than I deserve. I believe now I do fully and deeply appreciate all. Announcements? No. All that I have said, I have said to you and to none else. Last evening M. A. Donelly was married to Westcott, and they are to live in Boston. Never did I long more to see you.

You would strengthen me and do me a world of good. Can't you come out? Dora must come. I would not have had her lately on any account, for she would have worked herself to death, — but very soon we shall be in a better fix for help in the various departments, so do make her come; she will be of great service to us and we will not quite kill her. . . . I am grieved at W. H. C.'s long illness. Oh! how we need him.

Adieu
Marianne

The Whitehouses are discontented at the North American Phalanx. . . .

Friday, Dec. 12, 1845.

My dear Anna,

I have been so constantly occupied with various matters this week, that I scarcely remember what I said in my last letter to you; probably it was rather dismal and cheerless; but now we stand in clearer light, and I can give you a more encouraging statement. I have made C. K. N. promise to call and see you tomorrow, as he earnestly wishes to do, and I intend he shall be the bearer of this letter with its good tidings. We are not dead here, but live — our hearts are firm and true, our courage good, and our hands ready for action. I wish I could remember what I told you in my last, — it must have been the dark side of our affairs, I think, for then, I looked to the future with fear and trembling. We have had a most cheering meeting of the association on Wednesday evening. Fred was absent. Every one present was firm and determined, and *full of confidence* that we *shall* and *will* bring Brook Farm to success. There is no word of discouragement from anyone, — no thought of anything but going on together with our best efforts, — there was one heart, one soul, one opinion, and all the strength and hope that comes from such union. And yet our position was carefully and candidly examined in its worst aspects; every argument that had been heard against our success was brought up and looked at. How small and insignificant they all seemed compared with the great ends we have in view! We felt that to be influenced by them would be treachery to the cause. I do not believe a man or woman here (of any value to the cause) would leave Brook Farm now, excepting Fred. Our dear, good warm-hearted, devoted Fred, for whose stability we would once have wagered everything valuable to us, — "our Fred," as we loved to call him, — has (not in wisdom as I think, but in weakness) yielded to the influences that have been so long and steadily and resolutely at work upon him, yielded even to the changing of his convictions. Still he calls himself an Associationist — still declares that in civilization he shall work only for the cause, — but he says Brook Farm *must* come to naught, — he believes it is not founded on so high a basis as something else will be, and he will wait and work for that something. Oh! it is sad to see him so deluded. I tell him he is deceiving himself — that when he quits Brook Farm he will soon cease to work for the movement, — he will be chained faster and firmer in a civilized hell. Has he not chosen sadly? Does not your heart ache for him?

To return to our meeting. It was glorious. Everything was asked and answered in good spirit. Mr. Ripley read a letter which he had written to Mr. Brisbane, defining our position; and declaring our intention to go on here, on this spot, and our reasons therefor, which letter gave us much satisfaction. Then J. S. D. set forth clearly and at length, our present case, and the course of action the council had decided it would be best to pursue. He looked fearlessly at the strongest arguments which had been brought up in private conversation of late, against our chance of success, and showed how little they were really worth; that we must look at this movement in a higher point of view than a merely mercantile one, and be willing to be sustained by faith until the time comes when we shall be able to realize pecuniary success. After all this had been fully talked over, we had some very interesting conversation about the social atmosphere of the place, — the difficulty and importance of a cordial hospitality to strangers and newcomers, — the importance of cultivating a warm, genial, social feeling towards all. The tone of the meeting inspired us all, and especially our lecturers, John Orvis and Allen, who were to set off the next morning, for a fortnight's tour thru' Lynn, Marblehead, Gloucester, etc., with a view to procuring subscribers for the Harbinger, and ascertaining the amount of interest in the cause that may be relied on in that region. They will return at Christmas time, spend three or four days with us, then off again for many weeks, in another direction. May God inspire them, that their golden lips may utter divine words to the people, and kindle a fire in many hearts!

What a magnificent evening! I wonder how you are passing it. These are heavenly clear days that shine upon us now, are they not? How is it with you in Boston? Are you almost frozen? Our greenhouse is the most charming little spot that ever was. I wish more of the rich people in Boston would order bouquets now; Mr. K. could furnish really magnificent ones. It is a treat to go in there and enjoy one's self among the birds and flowers, and with the conversation of Mr. K., the presiding genius. I passed an hour there the other evening by moonlight, with the flowers. Our sickness seems to be all over. Mrs. P. leaves the Cottage tomorrow.[1]

I regret C. K. N.'s [2] departure more than I can tell. He has been always a conspicuous, or rather an important object in the picture to me. I can hardly think of Brook Farm without him. The sweet, sad youth! He will feel the change still more than we. Think of him in a city life, if you can. Oh! it will kill him, soul and body. Wherever he is, may God bless him and cheer him. I hope you will have a pleasant call from him. When shall I see Dora, when thee? Do write.

Ever yours
Marianne

Brook Farm, Dec. 31, 1845.

Dear Frank,

As the old year is almost gone, I will take this opportunity to wish you a happy new year. We have had a glorious winter day, cloudless and dazzlingly bright, very *cold*, but so tempting on the pure white snow, that one could hardly stay in doors. What kind of a day has it been to you? Busy, no doubt, and *figured* all over. The Archon had a letter from Allen, written to us all, in fine spirits and full of encouragement, and giving a glowing description of a storm they enjoyed at Rockport, — informing us also that they could not be with us till next Monday or Tuesday. We have had quite an interesting Fourier reading tonight, on Social Destiny. . . . Mr. Grant and Mr. Brisbane are expected here this week. John has had

[1] Mrs. Palisse. [2] Newcomb.

another letter from Eben Hunt, saying that the prospect for the music lectures in N. Y. is encouraging and the matter progresses. It will do if he does not go on till March. . . . Again a happy new year to you and good night.

Your affectionate sister
Marianne

Pilgrim H[ouse], March 1, 1846.

Thank you, dear Anna, for your two notes, and also for those imaginary, long and interesting letters you have written me lately — for I love to dwell in the thought of those who are near and dear to me. We have a fine Sunday, and if it be right to wish anything, most earnestly do I wish you were here. W. H. C. came last evening looking bright and cheerful: says he was better for coming out last Sunday. Of course we passed last evening at the Eyrie, till about nine o'clock. John and W. H. C. were together in John's room in earnest conversation, and Mrs. R. and I were similarly occupied in mother's room. I had really a very pleasant talk with her. Then we went down and had music till eleven.

The order of events today is yet unrevealed, probably will not be unlike last Sunday. If I get time, I'll add a line when night comes, to tell you. John O. has sent on a good letter, which will appear in the next Harbinger. . . . I have not had a line yet, but felt refreshed by reading this. Mr. Butterfield thinks we have not those numbers of the Harbinger which Mrs. Jarvis wants, — but if they can be found they will be sent to her. . . .

Tell Helen, Mr. Blake asks why she did not come out last evening. The dear girl, — I long to have her living here with you and the rest of us. Why is it, can you tell, that I, who am not near so good as either of you and am so much less worthy, should be here, when you cannot come? Association needs the choicest, but has to take up with what it can get. We have had this week what Lizzie calls an incursion of Cape Cod barbarians. Mr. Bacchus, two Pitchers, Mr. Bassett and Capt. Proctor. Also two Manchester men have come, with their wives, and one child.

Evening. Oh, Anna — such a holy, solemn afternoon! Mr. Channing spoke to us on devotedness to the cause; the necessity of entire self-surrender; of entire obedience to the will of God. He compared our work with others that have demanded sacrifice; that of the crusaders, that of the religious brotherhoods and sisterhoods. As the crusaders sacrificed so much to restore the tomb of the buried Lord, how much more ought we to sacrifice, whose work it is to restore the whole earth that it may become the dwelling place of the living Lord! And as the monks and nuns withdrew from the world, to be free from temptations and sin and to become pure — how much more need have we of earnest devotedness, whose work it is to regenerate and purify the world! He compared us too with the Quakers, who see God only in the inner light, whereas we, by our doctrine, are to see him in every thing, in the intellect, in every affection of the soul, every amusement, every act; with the Methodists, who seek to be in a state of rapture in their sacred meetings, whereas we should maintain in daily life, in every deed, on all occasions, a feeling of religious fervor; with the perfectionists, who are, he says, the only sane religious people, as they believe in perfection, and their aim is one with ours. Why should we, how dare we tolerate ourselves or one another in sin? He solemnly urged upon us no idleness, no halfwayness in our devotedness, but the entire surrender of all our powers to this work; nothing else can give success. Heaven help us and make us the better for his earnest, truth spoken words! — I've been writing a few lines by way of P.S. in Lucas's letter to Charles Newcomb. Was I presumptuous? Now I must to the Eyrie. How I regret Mary's departure, and so do we all.

Adieu.

Marianne

Brook Farm, Wed. a.m., March 4, '46.

Dearest Anna,[1]

I requested Frank to show you a hasty note I sent in to him this morning, announcing the burning of our Phalanstery, and as I know you are anxious for further particulars, I must with what poor words I can, attempt to put you in possession of them. The council meeting had just appointed a committee to superintend the finishing of the Phalanstery and had dispersed, when Mr. Salisbury, passing the building, saw a light in the upper part, and put his head into a window to learn the cause thereof. (Men had been at work there all day, and a fire kept up in the stove.) He found the room full of smoke, and ran instantly to the Eyrie and told Mr. Ripley, who was the first on the spot. Then came the sudden, earnest cry, "Fire! the Phalanstery!" that startled us all, and for a moment made every face pale with consternation. I was in my room, just about writing to Dora. I ran to the front of the house. Flames were issuing from one of the remote windows, and spreading rapidly. It was at once evident that nothing was to be

[1] This letter has been quoted in G. W. Cooke's *John Sullivan Dwight.*

done. It seemed but five minutes when the flames had spread from end to end. Men ran in every direction, making almost fruitless attempts to save windows and timber. The greatest exertions were made to save the Eyrie, which at one time was too hot to bear the hand, and even smoked. Our neighbor, Mr. Orange, went first upon the roof and worked like a hero, and not in vain. But the scene! Here words are nothing — Why were you not here? Would I could convey to you an idea of it. It was glorious beyond description. How grand when the immense heavy column of smoke first rose up to heaven! There was no wind, and it ascended almost perpendicularly, — sometimes inclining towards the Eyrie, — then it was spangled with fiery sparks, and tinged with glowing colors, ever rolling and wreathing, solemnly and gracefully up — up. An immense, clear blue flame mingled for a while with the others and rose high in the air, — like liquid turquoise and topaz. It came from the melting glass. Rockets, too, rose in the sky, and fell in glittering gems of every rainbow hue — much like our 4th of July fire-works. I looked upon it from our house till the whole front was on fire, — that was beautiful indeed, — the whole colonnade was wreathed spirally with fire, and every window glowing. I was calm, felt that it was the work of Heaven and was good; and not for one instant did I feel otherwise. Then I threw on my cloak and rushed out to mingle with the people. All were still, calm, resolute, undaunted. The expression on every face seemed to me sublime. There was a solemn, serious, reverential feeling, such as must come when we are forced to feel that human aid is of no avail, and that a higher power than man's is at work. I heard solemn words of trust, cheerful words of encouragement, of resignation, of gratitude and thankfulness, but not one of terror or despair. All were absorbed in the glory and sublimity of the scene. There was one minute, whilst the whole frame yet stood, that surpassed all else. It was fire throughout. It seemed like a magnificent temple of molten gold, or a crystallized fire. Then the beams began to fall, and one after another the chimneys. The end, where the fire took, being plastered, held out the longest, but in less than an hour and a half the whole was leveled to the ground. The Phalanstery was finished! Not the building alone, but the scenery around was grand. The smoke as it settled off the horizon, gave the effect of sublime mountain scenery; and during the burning, the trees, the woods shone magically to their minutest twigs, in lead, silver and gold. As it was to be, I would not have missed it for the world. I wanted here you and Channing, Frank, Orvis and Allen, Mary B. and Helen and all the absent who belong to us. You know not what you have lost. And I do assure you, the moral sublimity with which the people took it was not the least part of it. The good Archon was like an angel. Mrs. Ripley alone was, for half an hour, too much overcome to look upon it. People walked here from Roxbury, Dedham, Boston and Cambridgeport. Engines could not help us much. There was such a rush of the world's people to the Hive! We gave them what we could — made hot coffee, brought out bread and cheese and feasted about 200 of the fatigued, hungry multitude. Mr. Orange brought us provisions from his house and ran thro' the street for milk.

About midnight I wrote letters to Orvis and Allen,[1] for I thought they would be in agony for us, if they did not get their first intelligence directly from home. I had one short,

[1] Who were absent, lecturing.

sound sleep and was up early writing to Frank. I looked at the bare hill this morning, I must say, with a feeling of relief — there was an incumbrance gone. Heaven had interfered to prevent us from finishing that building so foolishly undertaken, so poorly built and planned, and which again and again some of us have thought and said we should rejoice to see blown away or burned down. It has gone suddenly, gloriously, magnificently, and we shall have no further trouble with it. Just what the effect will be to us, it is impossible now to tell. The contract was lately given into our own hands, and I suppose ours must be the loss. About $7000 had been spent on it. We must take deep to heart a good lesson. We have been thro' almost every other trial; now we have been thro' the fire. We needed this experience, and I pray we may come from it like pure gold. It leaves us no worse off than before we began it, and in some respects better. May Heaven bless to us the event. I feared it would look ugly, dismal and smutty this morning, but the ruins are really picturesque. A part of the stone foundation stands like a row of grave stones, — a tomb of the Phalanstery — thank God, not the tomb of our hopes! Charles Dana returned from New York an hour since, and I am happy to say, takes it as cheerfully as the rest of us. We breakfasted an hour later than usual today, and our hired carpenters have gone back to Dedham and I see no other change. The day is calm and beautiful, all goes on as usual. We look towards the hill and all seems like a strange dream. You can't think how it struck me last night towards the close of the fireworks when, after watching the constantly rolling, changing flames, for two hours, I looked up to the sky and saw Orion looking down so steadily, so calmly, reminding me of the unchanging, the eternal. I fear you can hardly read this, I have been obliged to scribble so fast.

Ever your loving friend
Marianne

P.S. If Frank don't come out tonight please show this to him.

Thursday evening, March 12, 1846.

Dear Frank,

I have intended to write to you before this time and yet I have nothing definite to say. We are still in cheerful hopeful trust, and in deliberation. If we can only take the right steps I am sure all will be right, but we have a difficult problem to solve. One thing seems sure, that we will not and cannot disband; the union is too firmly cemented together for that, — we stay or go, — live or die *together*. Today I received a long letter from Allen, a truly noble letter. He received the first intelligence of the fire from my letter, and felt the blow severely. But he writes cheerfully, trustfully and encouragingly — in a truly religious spirit. He feels, as we all do, that we cannot separate. Mrs. Ripley has had a letter from Mr. Kay. He is quite delighted that the Phalanstery is burned, (you know he always quarrelled with it); thinks we can now stand on true ground — says we *must* go on. He will be here the first day that he can — at least (he hopes) by the last of the month. Ally will come at any rate. . . .

We rejoice in John Orvis's return. He felt somewhat dismal at first, but that has passed away; 'tis no atmosphere here for despondency — and now, after a good night's rest, he is bright and hopeful. . . .

The council are in session this evening, holding earnest consultation. Oh! for wisdom — *that* is the gem beyond all price — the rarest in the universe. . . .

Ever yours
Marianne

Monday a.m., [*March, 1846*].

Dearest Anna,

I long to have you realize what a comfort your letters are to me and others. You are a good child to write them. Believe me they do us real good and we have needed them. It was delightful, too, to see Mary's[1] cheering face. How much I want you here! It is a solemn time with us. Last evening we had a meeting of the whole to consult about measures to be taken. If (*sub rosa*) I except Charles D. every voice is firm and strong to go on if possible, and I think we have the spirit to conquer impossibilities (almost). At some rate or other, in some way or other, we *will* go on (Heaven willing), but it may involve a change in our plans. We wish our friends abroad God speed in all their benevolent efforts in our behalf. Almost everything will depend upon the aid we receive, — it will be heavy for us to shoulder such a loss alone. We are hopeful, brave, determined — we are solemn — we mean to be considerate, careful, just and honest and honorable. We will do the right, if we can. Our eyes are open. Go to Fisher's this evening, you will see Mr. Ripley and others — Do write — and more of Fred. Do, *do* get into the omnibus and come out. Tell your father, I need you.

Marianne

[1] Mary Bullard.

Tuesday eve, March 17, [1846].

Dearest Anna,

I find so many of the friends who are most interested in the events of next Thursday evening, are so particularly desirous of your presence here, that I write again to urge it. Perhaps W. H. C. may have told you, if not I will tell you now a secret. It is to be an important evening. Keep it to yourselves, you and Helen and Mary, for the parties concerned do not wish it known here until the time comes. I invite you to a wedding.[1] So I suppose, for Fanny Macdaniel, when she told me the party was to be for Eunice, and earnestly asked me to get you and Helen and Mary here (all, if possible, but especially you), said I might guess what I pleased but not tell anybody but you. I expect we shall have a fine time. Give my love to Helen and Mary. Tell them about it, and how very, very delightful it will be to us all to have you all here, for we feel that you are all identified with us. Can't you manage all to be here? We can find some sleeping place for you all, and you can come out in the omnibus. I am looking for you, Anna, all the time, — perhaps I shall see you tomorrow.*

Mr. Ripley had a pleasant and bright, cheering letter from "Our John"[2] today. He says he has told the *exact truth* to the New York friends and they don't think our case nearly as bad as they expected; think we *must go on*, — relinquish readily whatever stock they have, — and are

* Please *all* count the *alls*.

[1] An unpublished letter in the Boston Public Library, from Charles A. Dana to John S. Dwight, dated Tuesday, March 1846, explains that he and Eunice Macdaniel had been privately married in New York and were to give a wedding party on Thursday evening.

[2] John S. Dwight.

ready to assist by a subscription as soon as our plan is struck. And I suppose it soon will be. Come as soon as you can, and again I ask that, if possible, you will all three be with us on Thursday evening. Tell Mary she promised me to come on all great occasions.

Yours lovingly
Marianne

I don't know that this secret has been revealed to mother or Fanny, so you must recollect when you come out, not to mention it.

Brook Farm, Tuesday eve, Mar. 17, '46.

My dear brother,[1]

Your letters are very delightful, especially the one Mr. R. received to day, and we rejoice that you are having so rich a time, but take care you don't get quite used up, or annihilated in that great City. You must have received Mrs. R.'s letter ere this, which I suppose gave you an account of the state of things here. I feel that we grow stronger and firmer all the time and are coming near to a decision upon our future plans. Probably the creditors will very soon be called together, and a settlement offered them. We shall tell them as the Archon says, that we are an obstinate set of chaps, — that they may, if they wish, take the property and sell it, but that this will not be for their interest, as we are determined to make it go yet, and believe that we can do it. We have men here willing to be responsible for the farm, men willing to be responsible for the shop, and so on, and we do mean, if it is a human possibility, to come to some success here. Charles still talks long in council, maintaining his view that it will be impossible to

[1] John Sullivan Dwight.

carry on any mechanical branches or agriculture, or to make any attempt towards an association. He would dismiss all but about twenty people, and have only a school and the Harbinger. Miserable! I wonder at the patience with which others can listen to it. I am told he is alone in his views, but I think he must hinder and perplex the council; I should like to have him take a journey for a few weeks and return when we got matters well settled. The probability is that we shall retain the sash and blinds, and the farm, and Harbinger, and get a good School. But upon what plan they will be retained is, as far as I can learn, yet unsettled.

Channing was gloriously strong last Sunday, and expressed exactly the view I have taken from the beginning, and the only one I can take, viz., — that we who have embarked here on this movement, have no right to desert it; we have no right to stop. If others choose to stop us, — why, that is another thing, — but we have no business to say the word ourselves. It would be a sin. It is and has been from the beginning so clearly a providential movement, — we who are here, have been so providentially led hither, — that I have not felt for a moment that we should dare think of abandoning it, and I have not heard anyone suggest the thing without a feeling of horror, as some criminal act. Channing spoke most cheeringly, said he felt a hope, a faith, such as he had never felt before, that we should go on, and go on to success. I wish you could have heard your choir, — they really did well, and you was scarcely missed.

I have had a noble, warm-hearted letter from Allen, full of sympathy, and hope and religious trust. We are expecting him daily. John Orvis came right home when he heard of the fire, and is strong and bright and firm in the faith. Mrs.

Ripley says that when she wrote to you, the tendency was towards giving up the property. It is now the contrary; we don't mean to give it up if we can avoid it, and the probability is that there will be no difficulty. It would be well if we can get the loan stock converted into partnership stock. It is encouraging to hear of the generosity of the New York friends whom you mention; we feel exceedingly grateful to all the noble souls who are willing to help us on in this work. Mr. Ripley says, stay till you get to the end of your rope, — as long as you can do us any good by staying. Tell the people to go on with the subscription; our plan will be forthcoming by and by. I think it will be pretty nearly as I said above, but we go on slowly and surely, — consuming more time in talk than I will ever believe to be necessary. Mr. Kay's letters are much liked, and I have no doubt it will be gratifying to him to know that we incline to his opinions, and find ourselves following his advice. I do hope you will bring him here when you return. He is *the* man of all men, whom I long to have on the spot. We want you here all the time. I hardly know whether you would help us most here or in New York, but I am certain that you are doing a good work for us where you are, so we feel reconciled to your absence. You are exactly the person to be in New York just after Charles Dana's visit, — and it seems to me a most providential circumstance. I think Channing told me he should probably not go to New York until May. He cannot leave *us* now, — he is determined to see our way clear, and when our plans are fairly settled, then he will make a most powerful appeal to the public in our behalf. Meantime the subscription is going on in Boston.

Your lectures! How I long to hear them. It is too

bad that you hadn't them *all* written before you left home; so you might give all your time to the overpowering attractions of the city. We see very favorable notices in the papers. Has your audience increased in number?

Oh! why can you not be with us tomorrow evening. We are to have a party at the Hive, with coffee, cake and speeches, to celebrate a great occasion, of which you shall hear more hereafter. Channing will be here, and I have sent for Frank, Mary, Anna and Helen. I am quite ashamed of such an uninspired letter, but the fact is my head aches too badly for any thought, and I am not just in the mood for writing, and yet I thought you ought to hear. . . . Don't get worn out with excitement there, for we shall have a plenty of work for you here when you come. Farewell.

Affectionately
Marianne

Sat. eve., [*Spring, 1846*].

My dear Anna,

I begin on this little piece of paper, because it is all my mother can find for me, and the storm drove me to the Eyrie, instead of to the Pilgrim, and what is more, it sent me around by way of the Cottage! Of all things I should love to have you here to talk with this evening. How much better it would be than this writing! The storm reconciles me somewhat to your absence, whilst it makes me desire your presence. The general council are in session and Channing with them. Every evening they hold deliberative meetings, and will continue to do so till they have agreed upon a course of action, when it will be proposed to the association. John Orvis says there is a deep hope in his heart that all will come out well; he gave me a full account today of their last evening's discussion, and really it promises well. I think we shall decide upon combining a thorough educational course with some industrial departments, printing the Harbinger, farming, etc. We shall get upon a sure basis yet. It is true our affairs don't stand so well, by a great deal, as we could desire, but we hope to find they are not past mending. Mr. Kay, our old friend, a great business character, thinks we can and shall retrieve ourselves. He is *glad* of the late calamity — thinks it will give us the only possible chance we could have had of turning our attention to the educational department and making it what it should be. He is more hopeful for us than ever. You ask how matters got into this fix. I will tell you — as well as I can. The debts mostly or wholly were incurred along in the commencement before it was a Fourier Association and are mostly due to people who loaned the money out of pure interest in the cause, and from a desire to see the experiment tried, and the money would not be called for. They are no trouble; they give us no anxiety — except that we have the interest to pay on them, which is a burden we long to be free from. Five or six hundred dollars would pay off all our pressing debts. It has been too much the practice here to push matters on too fast. The school was almost given up (at a time when we depended on it for support) in order to rush into various industrial, mechanical branches, and these have failed to support us. It might have been foreseen, but the whole was driven on by a few individuals, who have kept the management and knowledge of affairs too much to themselves. We should have waited till some mechanical department was able to support us, before we permitted the decline of the school. The result of the last year was, that we made not enough to defray the expenses of the year by 500 dollars. But then we were unfortunate. The smallpox cost us more than that. . . . Mr. Hatch's management and misconduct sunk us more than that — so that this $500 minus need not be completely discouraging. This is dry business and I let it go. We, of course, must now ascertain exactly the amount of our indebtedness and see how we can treat honorably with our creditors. We had trusted to the increased means which the Phalanstery would afford us for enlarging our business and making it profitable. We have never had capital enough to lay out in any department, to carry it on to advantage.

With regard to Fred — Too much has perhaps been said and too much notice taken of so small a matter — for it really *is* small, tho' his imagination has made a mountain of a mole hill. As I said before, Fred knows Charles D.'s manner too well to care one iota for it, and it is little in him to be so aggrieved by anything Charles could or did say. Mrs. Ripley, John and others regretted that Charles wrote the letter, because they did not like the tone of it, — still they did not think it a matter of great importance as it contained the truth, tho' boldly stated. I believe that all you write me of Fred is no more than I have heard him say. You see he quibbles more than he reasons, — his mind is diseased on the subject and most sincerely do I pity him. I am sorry to hear that he sent a long document to the Council last evening, which Mr. R. tells me is very insulting — I have not yet seen it. He sent to John O. with a few lines to him, saying that he sent it to him because he was determined to have the Council hear it, and he was afraid that if he sent it to Mr. R. he would pocket it and not be willing to produce it before the Council. What think you of this? Poor Fred! I believe the less said to him the better. Every word exasperates him more. If his mind could only rest awhile upon something else, it might do him good. John O. says he will write him a good loving letter.

And now shall I tell you something of a certain deep joy there is in my heart, giving a tone and strength to all my other emotions? Or shall I wait till I see you. Oh! I will *wait*, for you are coming out here this very week. . . . All that I have been writing to you comes so far short of the whole that is to be said, that it seems one sided as I read it over — we must talk. I cannot find that anyone here has any ill feeling or any exasperation whatever towards Fred. He has himself created a great hubbub about his own ears — we don't make it — we believe that when left to himself he will come to his senses and be as much ashamed of the steps he has taken, and the hue and cry he is making, as his friends here are now ashamed of him. We pity him and are sorry to have him so unhappy, and I would gladly see him more manly and noble than to fight so hard for his rights, were he ever so right. But I repeat, he would not be so inconsistent, so contradictory, so unjust, so unfriendly, so revengeful, if he knew what he is about. He has worked himself up to a pitch of insanity on this point, and I can't see that we could have helped it and we, of course, blame him. I see he has influenced you somewhat, but I shall tell you the whole when we meet, — and I beg of you to consider if he will not be soonest cured by having his mind led off in another direction for awhile. It seems to me even loving words (as is usual in insanity) have made him worse. . . .

(*The end of this letter is missing*)

Brook Farm, Sunday. Mar. 22, 1846.

My dear Anna,

It has been quite a trial to me to get along all this while without seeing you. All the letters I have written have been so entirely unsatisfactory to me, that each one has but made me long the more to have a talk with you. However, written words, are to me far better than none. My note, inviting you to the wedding, went to Boston in Mr. Monday's pocket, and came back to me yesterday. He forgot to deliver it, — no wonder you was puzzled at the one that followed it! The party — the wedding party went off very well — very pleasantly indeed. I think about a dozen .of our best people preferred to stay away. Others of us felt and thought, that altho' the privacy of the wedding and other circumstances were unpleasant, or perhaps worse than that, this public announcement was, at least, a right step; it was best to go, and in kindness and justice make it as agreeable as we could. I had a little talk with W. H. C. He did not seem to see any cause for our feeling as we do about it, — said he knew all the circumstances, etc. Well, — I doubt if he does know all, — at any rate, he don't know Eunice, tho' I would not tell him this. Fanny M. has put me in possession of the whole, as she understands it, and gives me liberty to tell *you*, — but I will not write it. Wait till we meet. I am glad, as it was to be, that they are married, — for they seem very happy; Charles now talks brightly and cheeringly of Brook Farm. This wedding party, and the Hive party I mentioned were one and the same thing. Dear Mary! her letter charms me. How much I feel for her, and how I long to see her. . . . Oh! tell her Brook Farm is her true home, where she shall have love and sympathy and the true freedom that these give, —

will she not come? — where she shall find an aim in life worth the living for, and demanding the exercise of her best and noblest powers, now almost dormant, — will she not think of it? Tell her John writes us very beautiful and very cheering letters, — finds the New York friends warm in our behalf and determined that they will help us; they will not hear of our stopping (a thing we have no thought of doing). His lectures are spoken of very enthusiastically. We hear, by a private letter, that he will probably have to repeat them there, and also in Philadelphia. His going there and just at this time, is one of those providential things that are ever occurring to us. It will do Association good in more ways than one. . . .

I have received a letter from Fred. To call it by its right name, it is the *most insulting* thing he has written yet; tho' I take some comfort from it for his sake, as it seems to be written in a more quiescent mood than the other letters. He is less excited, but seems to feel so ugly and revengeful. Oh! when will he chain up those devils, and listen to the still, small voices of his good angels? Of course I shall not answer such a letter, — as Mr. Ripley says, "I am not a man to fight a duel." I gave it to John O., who is now writing to Fred. I wish you could see the beautiful tea rose bud John has brought me. I've been making two or three drawings from it. Oh! poor little undeserving me! How many duties I am called to in this world, for which I feel myself unworthy and unfitted and yet know that the calling is from God, and must be obeyed unhesitatingly and with grateful joy. I am filled with new, deep joy, — a sad joy, too, — for I never realized as I now do, my shortcomings, — and the absolute necessity of becoming much better and wiser than I am. Help me all you can.

Last evening, we had here a new flowering of the tree of life that seems to have taken such deep root in this spot, in spite of the soil. Our friend and associate, W. H. Cheswell, wishing to celebrate the anniversary of his arrival at this Eden, invited everybody to attend his regular dancing school. I felt very unlike it, had been almost ill with the headache all day, — but as friend Cheswell has always looked with a jealous eye upon the aristocratic element, John thought it would be best to go, and persuaded me into it, and right glad we are that we went. The dancing went off in fine style, — it could not have been better — and about ten o'clock, two by two, we were all marched out of the dining hall into the parlors, to await the setting of a table. When notice was given, each gentleman took his lady and we marched back again and seated ourselves at a table, which extended thro' the centre of the room from end to end, and offered us the tempting luxuries of hot coffee, cake, crackers and cheese. After partaking of these dainties, Charles Dana rose and announced that he would read the toasts that had been prepared for the occasion. They were very excellent, and some of them not a little amusing. The different groups were toasted, from the printing group to the plain sewers, and individuals called upon for speeches. These were ready and admirable. We had fun and wit and poetry and sober good sense, and earnestness and solemnity. There was a new consecrating of each and all to our work here at Brook Farm, — a pledging of the groups to faithful, devoted, needful action, and the very heartiest expression of hope and faith and union. The one discordant note that has sounded in our ears lately came round into harmony, and thunders of applause burst forth as Charles Dana, with recovered strength and energy, expressed his deep faith that the cause of Association and the work of Association must and would to some extent be carried on here at Brook Farm. The Archon, unluckily, was not present, and says he wants to have it over again! (It was such a meeting as never happens but once.) Charles Dana and John Orvis were the only persons present, of our usual speakers. No matter, — indeed, all the better, — for there was no restraint, — anybody could get up and, in his way, say the good word; and I do say it was one of the very best parties I ever attended. Do tell Mr. Channing, if you see him, that I would have given the world to have had him present, or perhaps behind the scenes; it would have done his heart so much good, to have seen this new development of the good spirit that is working in us and binding us together in strength. In truth, we *are* a *Phalanx*. Tonight we are to have a meeting of the whole to discuss the measures proposed by the Council, and which I believe don't involve much change in our organization. How liked you Allen's letter? Will you send it right back, as there is something in reference to hoe handling, etc., that our farmers want to see at once. . . . Farewell. Love to all.

Your affectionate
Marianne

My 60 flowers for J. A. Lowell, Esq., were finished and sent to him yesterday, for which he returned at once thirty dollars.

April 7, [*1846*].

Dear Frank,

I write to tell you that our gentlemen brought home very good news this evening. They went to Boston intending to make this proposition to the creditors, viz. that they would convert $7000 of debts into partnership stock. They did better for us than this, relinquished entirely $7000 of debts, each creditor giving up a sum in proportion to the amount of his claim. The next proposition was, that we should be exempted from paying any interest for the next year. This was agreed to; and after that, for the next four or five years. If (after allowing for our board and clothing) any profits remain, they are to be divided equally between us and the creditors. After that time we may make any new arrangement. Thus you see we are better off than we expected or even hoped. Now let us be thoughtful and careful. Mr. Morton was present and perfectly ready to assent to any thing we asked, and he expressed his growing faith in Association and his interest in Brook Farm. . . .

Good night.
Marianne

Tell Anna the news herein contained.

Brook Farm, April 19, '46.

Dearest Anna

How I have neglected you of late! and have been compelled to do so and yet I have a thousand things to talk with you about. . . . Today the weather is so beautiful, so summer-like! I took a little ramble alone this morning and gathered a few anemones — the first I have seen, which I send to you. This afternoon I have had a little walk with John [1] — we went into the Pine Woods and both of us longed to have you with us. . . . I cannot tell you how perfectly delicious here — balmy — the air is, how sweetly the birds sing, how beautiful and fresh the earth is after

[1] John S. Dwight.

last night's showers. But I must leave the summer air, that has been all day breathing to me sweetest memories of last year, and hopes deep and earnest of the future, and talk of other matters. First, let me tell you how I am writing. Here in the Eyrie parlor, — John [1] at the piano, Channing and others sitting around the room; thus am I obliged to steal time to talk with you, for I cannot bear to lose this music and this presence. Would they might inspire me as they ought, to write you a worthy letter, but no — it cannot be, for I shall talk on very practical matters.

We are now starting in what appears a common sense way; we have reduced our plans somewhat, but I trust a higher ideal is before us than ever. One thing is certainly very encouraging and to me is really providential. How is it that the people who are not calculated to help us, who, tho' good in their way, yet lack that refinement which is indispensable to give a good tone to the place, do actually withdraw in the pleasantest manner, wholly unasked, and without any chance of feeling that their withdrawal is desirable to us? I cannot call it chance. God wills it. God means something by it. We have lately felt it really necessary that certain people should leave, — we have not known how to bring it about. Our friends, the Cheswells, for instance; well, all at once, comes a call to them from abroad, — a better prospect opens to them outside the camp, than from within, and they have gone to enjoy it, — bidding us adieu with kind feelings and some regrets which indeed are mutual. Mrs. Ryckman and Jeanie, too, are gone, but we hope some time to have Mrs. R. back again. Also Mr. Drew is to depart tomorrow. In those changes there is something trying to our feelings, — but they are

[1] John S. Dwight.

well, and we are thankful that they have come so pleasantly about. Those of us who will be left are capable of improving by living together, and feel very closely drawn together. We feel, too, our brotherhood with those who have gone, — but it always seemed to me a great mistake to admit coarse people upon the place. Now we need not fear subjecting our pupils to evil influences from such quarters. Indeed, I see not why we cannot now offer them as good or better moral influences than could be found at any other boarding school. My interest now must centre in the school. I do know what a good school is. I know well why we have not had a good one here, and I see clearly that we can easily have the very best, and I am solemnly determined to use my utmost efforts to bring it about. I have offered myself to the work, — have just been elected chief of the teachers' group which gives me, together with Mrs. R. (chief of the educational service), and indeed more than she, the superintendence of the school. Her health requires that I should give her this relief and I enter upon the duties with alacrity and cheerfulness, — with diffidence to be sure, and yet with confidence, for I am most fully determined that it shall be a good school. And then think what aid I can command. The Ripleys, Charles Dana, John S., Fanny, Miss Russell, etc. Indeed, it shall be done, heaven helping.

The change we make in our organization will secure to each group greater independence than before; each will transact its own business, make its own sales and purchases, etc. We need money to invest in some departments and for this purpose a subscription is now going on. We feel that we have a right to call upon civilizees to help us with their money to accomplish what we can towards building up a true system of life. Some help has come to us and undoubtedly more is at hand. For the school I don't mean to lay out much at present (provided I can get it) but I do need twenty-five or thirty dollars very much indeed and immediately, for furniture for the room, and I trust our financial department will be able to appropriate this at least. It would be well to have fifty dollars more towards getting together an industrial establishment for the boys. Mr. Cushing of Watertown said in a note to Mr. Roelker that tho' he might not be able to do what the association needs, he would be glad to aid the contribution, and should be very happy to see Mr. Ripley. Mr. R. intends to go out there tomorrow. . . .

My room is sweet with the fragrance of a few wild flowers (I forgot to tell you at the top of this page that I have come home to my room). I send them to you and Fanny. . . . Oh, Anna! Make a last, desperate effort to come out here and live. It will do you good; it will restore you to life and health. Is there no possible way of impressing this upon your father? Mrs. R. has been quite ill, and tho' better, is still far from well. Mrs. Dana also is ill, but recovering. Tell Fanny that ere long she must pass a day with me. I wish she could see our beautiful white doves fly up into my hand, and eat breadcrumbs therefrom. They are perfectly tame and would fly into hers just as readily. I am not going to give up painting on account of the school, but shall be obliged to give less time to it. . . .

Farewell.

Marianne

Brook Farm, Aprl. 24, 1846.

My dear Anna,

Your letter is so full of spirit that it quite inspired me and I felt no little disappointment that Mr. Ripley should have discouraged your plan. My feeling and I think the general feeling here is, if any friends of the cause see fit to put into operation any plans they may have for helping it on, thro' aid given to this particular movement, let them do so, and Heaven bless their efforts. I sometimes wish people would do so without asking or consulting us in the least. With regard to the proposed gathering in the Faneuil Hall. I do not doubt but a great degree of determination and active, untiring zeal and energy (such as your letters tell me you at least have) on the part of several individuals, would do a good work for us. But where are they who have it? Particularly where are the ladies? Where is the *one*, the Mrs. Chapman of Association, around whom might be a rallying. I believe that centre is wanting. Anti-slavery fairs and fetes are supported by wealth; where are the people of wealth who are enlisted in the Association cause? I see that you have entered warmly into this project, and I don't like to discourage you. It seems to me when I read your letter that it must go, — but it would require tremendous effort. Think of it. You are not equal to it. The excitement, the fatigue would be enough to kill you and for your sake, I do indeed veto the proceeding. If it should fail, think how very ridiculous! I like better the old plan of a rural fete by and by. That with addresses from the gentlemen you named, with music, refreshments, etc. it appears to me, would realize something.

Mr. Channing spoke of addressing Mr. Clarke's people in our behalf. I fear the effort will be too much for his health, and moreover, would not an appeal from Mr. C. himself have really more influence over his people? If it would be so, can't you bring this about? I wish Mr. Parker would address his people. He is their idol, and a word from him may be of great avail. New scholars have not come yet, but our little school is going on finely, — and now I will unhesitatingly promise as good instruction, as good influences in every way, as I believe can be had elsewhere. We must eventually depend on pupils from some distance who will stay with us summer and winter, and I earnestly wish that for this summer, we might fill up with scholars from Boston and the neighborhood, should they stay but a short time. I think this very desirable, as we shall not be likely to get any number of distant pupils for some months. Advertising costs too much money for us to run any great risk in that way. I wish some of the friends who know well the strength of our educational department here, now that it stands up again and means to assert itself, would put notices in daily papers, — these are often of some avail. Our school has lost reputation abroad, not from want of talent here to conduct it, but because that talent has been diverted from it. I want people to know that it is turning back again with full and steady force. I like Frank Peabody very much, and am glad that he seems so well and happy here. At last our general plan of operations is fixed. The farm and the school are to be the main departments. The greenhouse is to have some additional force. The printing is to be carried on as before, with the addition of a handpress to be kept constantly at work, which will bring a handsome profit. The shoemaking is to be abolished, — one hand to be employed in mending. The tailoring to be given up, except so far as to make garments for people on the place, and do any work that may *offer* from abroad, but none will be sought. It is thought more profitable to give the tailoring force to the farm, which needs help exceedingly. The shop we will let if we can. Hereafter we are to take note of results rather than of hours — a change in which I heartily rejoice. . . .

Oh! the sweet epigæa! Many thanks therefor. Before I opened the box, I made up my mind that it contained that sweet flower. It is too late for me to write more. . . .

Affectionately
Marianne

Brook Farm, Tuesday evening, [*July 28, 1846*].

Dear Frank,

I get no time to write by daylight, and find myself too tired, or lamp-light too uncomfortable to undertake it in the evening. . . . There is little to tell you by way of news. Tomorrow Mr. Kleinstrup and Mr. Palisse start for N. Y., and will visit the North American Phalanx. Mr. K. is really determined to leave. I fear the Palisses will soon go, and the Mondays, — tho' they don't say anything about it. I must tell you, with a deep feeling of disappointment, (tho' I believe we are in God's hands and feel resigned to what must come) that I see little reason to hope for any success here. I think we might have it, if the people were persistent, — but there is a general discouragement and want of hope, — a willingness, it seems to me to let the thing come to naught so far as an industrial association is concerned. It seems to me that our secret central council, our leaders here, don't even care to have an industrial association, — don't believe it can be, and aim only to carry on the school and the Harbinger. I don't believe the school and Harbinger will support the place, if people enough remain to make the life anything like as associative as it has been. They want to let out the farm. Well — I don't know — my hope all along has been in the people; if the wise, the good and true think it their duty to quit, how or what shall I hope for Brook Farm? Oh! there is something rotten in Denmark depend upon it. I do what I can now — what my duty may be ere many weeks I know not. You may think this desponding. I am not so. I don't mean to be so even if I see this beloved Brook Farm, this adopted home, draw to an end, — but enough of this. . . .

With much love
Marianne

Thursday a.m., [*July, 1846*].

Dear Frank,

How much I regretted last evening that you had not come out then instead of the evening before. We had music at the Eyrie and you could not but have enjoyed yourself. As it is, with your bed on the floor and all, I fear you are only the worse for coming. We shall have another meeting to night. (Oh dear! I dread it and yet there is no reason why I should, except the discomfort of a warm evening.) This proposed plan of independent groups, — this return to *civilized* industry, — this dereliction from *principle* (as it seems to me) meets with scarce any approbation. John and Mr. Ripley seem almost alone to have faith in it, as a thing that will serve even to keep us together. It is sad to think what arguments are brought for this, as the result of our associative life. "It will be a spur to industry — people will exert themselves more when they are to have the benefit themselves, than when the money is going into the association"! What a comment upon the truth and devotion with which they take hold of the cause!

The fact is, as John wrote to Mr. Kay, we have three classes here, but I do not consider their relations to each other in the same light that he does. 1st, the *promulgators* of the doctrine, — they are represented by Charles Dana (who probably will not stop here long, whatever arrangements we may make). To this class belong the Ripleys, Danas and Macdaniels. They give assurance (as does also John S.) that they would not, on any account, enter an industrial association in these days, — nor are they particularly interested in the life here. They are working for a far future but don't believe in trying now to make their lives conform to the principles of association. I should call them *amateur* associationists. They have taken the doctrine into their heads more than into their hearts, else it *must* manifest itself in actual life, in daily deeds. 2d, the class which John represents, who would be here for the *life* we have led together, — they are interested in *promulgation* also, but care little for associated industry, — indeed John don't believe in it, except as something to be attempted by and by. Perhaps Miss Russell and our Fanny come in here (tho' Fanny's views are hardly settled enough for me to class her anywhere). 3d, the class who are for trying *now* to live together in associated industry, — they are interested in *promulgation*, — and love the life here as dearly as any, and also they must, they *will* if possible have the life, by the only possible way which can produce it, viz., by associative industry. To say who comprise this class, I should have to name almost every person not mentioned above. They are by far the majority — they have, as I think, the completest view, — they are thorough-going — they would be true outwardly and inwardly to the principles they have embraced. Lizzie

Curson, J. Orvis and I seemed to meet in a plan yesterday, which gives me the only ray of hope I have lately had for Brook Farm. As the Ripleys and John will not associate in industry with others, and as John believes a civilized school wholly incompatible with Association, let them take (as they have proposed doing) the school and Harbinger, and carry them on as independent branches, and make as much money as they can, — and let them pay the rest of us, who will go on as an Association, board for themselves and scholars. We then will make the farm (as a farm ought ever to be) the pivotal branch, — with a dozen good men it will do well. The greenhouse perhaps can be used as a forcing house in winter, to raise cucumbers and tomatoes to sell for a high price. The school will hire me, and I can paint, and we must retain as many as we shall need in the domestic work and no more. We must start fair and square, — so many of us are earnest and truly devoted, — and go on safely with our eyes open, seeing our way Along. What think you of it? I believe such a plan might go and must go. I think (if people are not in too much despair to believe that any thing could save us) that this will meet with universal approbation. Fanny Mac is delighted with it. I hear Mrs. Ripley is rather pleased — now if it will only suit her ladyship! Mr. Channing says it is perfectly fair to ask them to consent to this, — and they have declared that they will not have anything to do with the school, except as an independent branch. This will secure to them here a continuance of the pleasant life, which certainly would be destroyed by their plan of civilized labor and individual competition. It would secure to us their society, — it seems to me the only way of uniting us — the only salvation. *Can* we do it? — Shall we have the *courage*, the *perseverance*, the *industry*, the self-sacrifice, that will be demanded? I am ready to try.

(No signature)

[*October 17, 1846*]

Dear Frank,

The greatest objection to our having company on Sunday is that we have so little opportunity for any talk with you, — we enjoyed Harriet's visit very much, but felt that we had scarcely seen *you*. I thought certainly to have written to you this week, but the days have been busy with the autumn leaves, and painting rather more steadily than of late has affected my eyes so that I have not dared to write in the evening, lest I should be obliged to be idle the next day. The country is magnificent, I never knew it more so, and the weather fine. I only wish you could be out here all the time just now, to enjoy with us the beauties of the dying year. I have gathered fine leaves on Oak Hill this week, (hope we shall go there tomorrow) and have met with very good success (for me) in painting them. Mr. Monday, Mother and I went one day after cranberries, — found them in great abundance but were hurried home by approaching rain, with about 6 quarts apiece.

And now Frank, as I have come to the clear conviction that it is a real fact, and no imagination of mine, I will tell you that I am actually thinking of perpetrating marriage about Thanksgiving or Christmas time (probably the latter). I do wish most sincerely that this information may give you real pleasure, and if you look at it in its true light, I have not any doubt but it will. It would have seemed to me, a year and a half ago, the strangest thing that could have happened on the face of the earth, — now, it seems to me the most natural, and a step so clearly directed by

Heaven, made so plainly the path of duty, that it seems to me inevitable. We know of no reason that could be urged for deferring it, except the unsettled state of things here, and poverty. It has been already deferred from these reasons and we think it should not be so any longer. — Matters will very likely be always unsettled here, so long as Brook Farm exists, and as to poverty, that ought not to be made an obstacle to a true relation. It is a very different thing from what it would be, if one or both of us were incapable of taking care of themselves. I have no fear on that score. We shall not need much money to start with. Shall be content if we can furnish our room, and have everything of our own, however plain or humble. John will have (probably) about $75.00 and I shall make by my paintings a small sum for myself, and we calculate that about $100 will fit us out very comfortably for Brook Farm. Of course the future is quite uncertain, the fate of Brook Farm is uncertain. What John will conclude to do in the spring, I do not yet know. He has two or three plans. This winter, he will probably be gone considerably on lecturing tours, — and he feels very unwilling to go off again as a single man. He wants the settled, home feeling that marriage will give. It has not been from secretiveness or want of confidence that I have said nothing of all this before. It has been partly from our unsettled plans, and partly from the fact that the relation between John and myself has grown up so gradually, that there have never been any crises to date from. Moreover I believe that such things tell themselves. — My time grows short, and I must wind up my letter rather reluctantly. . . .

Affectionately your sister

Marianne

Wednesday evening, December 15, 1846.

My dear Anna,

I have referred Mr. Channing to *you* to inform him of my plan for Christmas eve,[1] but I do not know, now that I have thought more of it, that I have ever said much to you about it — in fact I have not had time to define it clearly to myself. You cannot think how disappointed I feel that there was no opportunity this evening for me to talk with Mr. C. . . .

You know we wish very much to have a religious exercise, connected with the rite, which is in itself most solemnly religious, and I want you to learn how Mr. C. feels about this, — if it would be agreeable to him, and how it could be managed. I believe that whatever he would like or think best could not fail to meet our wants and gratify our feelings. Therefore I wished to talk with him about it, thinking he might make some suggestion. This has occurred to me, — to have the parlors decorated for Christmas. To open the evening with music suited to the occasion, which should be followed by the ceremony — the great event of the evening. This to be followed by music again perhaps, something solemn and joyful. Then an address, a serious religious address to the people from Mr. C. (a Christmas discourse or what he likes) — then music, which shall be a transition between the preceding and a social party which shall succeed. This is my general idea about it. I would give the people pleasure and something more than pleasure, — deeper and better, and for this I want the sermon, and sacred music. And all the people here want it I do believe. Of course, I mean if Mr. Channing likes it. I can't think what would be pleasanter or better for us than

[1] For her wedding with John Orvis.

music (particularly, if Mary[1] comes) and the voice of the good friend, the religious teacher, whom we all love so much. I know nothing that could *unite* us so truly, and socially we have been, by our late arrangements, somewhat separated. Well, Anna — it is late, and I will say no more. Oh! I shall be so rejoiced (and so will John) to have Mr. C. here! . . .

Good night.
Ever your dear friend
Marianne

Thursday. Good morning, dear Anna. I awake bright and well. Yesterday I must have been very tired. I would like, on *that* evening, as in some of the olden times, that we should all feel, tho' but for a while, the sentiment of universal unity glowing in our souls.

Our parlor carpet was made and put down yesterday p.m. The couches come on next. If you would have a room furnished out of nothing, apply to Brook Farmers! In haste for breakfast.

Marianne

Brook Farm, Sat. eve., Mar. 29, [*1847*].

Dearest Anna,

. . . This p.m. I had a letter from John,[2] written yesterday. He has been having a nice time in Providence. Audiences larger than he has found elsewhere, — interest considerable. Charlie Newcomb wrote to Lucas that he spoke with great effect on Thursday p.m. They are to have a thorough convention there in two or three weeks — want Channing, Ripley and Allen. The people volunteer

[1] Mary Bullard. [2] John Orvis.

to pay the expenses. Brisbane was there Thursday evening — C. N. says his picture[1] enchanted all eyes. John made his home at Mr. Burgess's where Amelia Russell is now staying. The Burgesses are her intimate friends, and are interested in Association. John was to be at Pawtucket tonight, and probably will not be home for ten days to come. Ten *long* days — well, God speed the good work! I only wish that I were worthy to have a hand in it, — it is a great trial to me to feel so left out as I now do, — and yet I see hardly anything that I can do just now. But I am ready to fall into my place, (if there be any for me) wherever I can find it.

Oh, Anna! It is sad to think of the greenhouse plants being sold off. It is sad to see Brook Farm dwindling away, when it need not have been so. How it has struggled against all sorts of diseases and accidents, and defects of organization! With what vitality it has been endowed! How reluctantly it will give up the ghost! But is it not doomed to die by and by of consumption? Oh! I love every tree and wood haunt — every nook and path, and hill and meadow. I fear the birds can never sing so sweetly to me elsewhere, — the flowers can never greet me so smilingly. I can hardly imagine that the same sky will look down upon me in any other spot, — and where, where in the wide world shall I ever find warm hearts all around me again? Oh! you must feel with me that none but a Brook Farmer can know how chilling is the cordiality of the world.

But I am ready for anything that must be. I can give all up, knowing well that a more blessed home than we can

[1] His imaginary picture of the organization of a Fourier Phalanx, perhaps accompanied by the actual picture of a projected Phalanstery reproduced on p. 68 of this volume.

imagine will yet be prepared for humanity. No words can tell my thankfulness for having lived here, and for every experience here, whether joyful or painful. It certainly is very unusual for me, and I think it may be quite wrong, to look for less in the future than we have derived from the past, but it does seem as tho' in this wide waste of the world, life could not possibly be so rich as it has been here. This is a fact, however, that tho' our state here for some months past, has been on many accounts, very disagreeable, and very little to my taste, yet life is more rich to me at this very time than ever; my inner life is more true and deep, — but I want a field for external action, a very small and humble one, of course, but I want something. I wait very patiently, however, and certainly find enough to be busy about. . .

Dearest, believe me ever your friend
Marianne

NOTE ON THE TEXT

In editing the foregoing letters, I have wished above all to present a readable text. Hence:

(1) Abbreviations not quickly intelligible have been expanded.

(2) Capitalization has been regularized in accordance with modern usage. A few changes have been made in spelling and punctuation.

(3) Dashes and underlinings, a natural feature of familiar letter writing, have been retained only when they appear to be used with definite intention. Underlined words have been set in italics.

(4) Passages which are repetitions or which have nothing to do with the situation at Brook Farm have been omitted.

(5) Dates supplied by other hands than those of Marianne Dwight are inclosed in square brackets.

A. L. R.

APPENDIX

A READING OF FOURIER'S CHARACTER BY ANNA PARSONS

I don't believe this a very gay person, tho' he gives me this inclination to laugh. Isn't there a deep sadness in the character? He seems one who *sported* with misery — brings the laugh of the *insane* to my mind. Isn't there great resolution, great firmness? I'm almost afraid of it — there seem such contradictory elements in the character. Unless you know him intimately you will not think what I say true — there is a lightness, suavity, agreeableness of manner very different from the depths of his character. A person of a *great deal of power.* Had the power of putting aside what torments and troubles him in the depths, of seeming, of being at ease for the time. Has *great* activity of intellect. One who hates oppression — am not certain he would not be likely to oppress — would not intend it, but might be likely to impose his views and plans upon others. I feel much more like having an agreeable conversation with you all than like reading. I get this feeling from the letter. Feel like making many quotations and not particularly apt ones. I never could talk so fast as his moods would change — has great flippancy and great depth — one you'd always find just where you didn't expect. If I laugh, it makes me sad, — if I'm sad, it makes me laugh. Had a great deal very noble and generous —

Would not he do things perfectly unaccountable? *vile* almost, — *Satanic?* [*Laughing*] The image that comes to my mind is a little *condensed devil*, squeezed into the corner of his heart, and oozing out.

A very difficult character to read. I'm afraid to go into the depths, — there's such a variety in it (something of the chameleon nature). Had great self will and great imagination.

[*Here she called for another letter of opposite character — said this was French. Holding the second letter.*] This is a more orderly character. The impression the first now gives me is of much excellent matter not well arranged. I have the feeling of trying to arrange many promiscuous things, a difficulty of classifying. I have to hunt 'round for what I wish. The second seems a more noble, dignified and staid person than that. [*After a pause*] As I hold this [*the second*] I like *that* better — more *heart* in that. It seems to me this man's heart would be a square, — that [*the first*] heart-shaped. I like this first person now, — has a great deal of real, genuine worth. Has struggled much with his own nature. I *respect* him too. He lives up to his convictions more than most of us. These two persons would come to conclusions very differently. The first would jump to them. If the truth were represented to his mind, he would receive it at once. They make me think of the hare and tortoise.

[*She laid aside the second letter, and took again the first.*] This is a *very earnest* man, a man of *warm* zeal — Has *great love* of the race — hearty. *Humanity* sounds in my ears continually since I've taken up the letter this time. He interests me very much indeed. Wish I were stronger that I might do him justice. Sometimes I should incline to laugh at him, — sometimes to laugh with him, but in my heart of hearts, should have a deep reverence and love for him.

Did you ever see him when he got hold of a new idea? I should like to get up and dance around the room — he's so delighted when he has got it fixed just right. He is *so* pleased, *so* happy! Seems a joyous old man. Doesn't he love children? Seems like a child himself sometimes — now like a child, then like a man in full vigor of life. Seems like a *dear old soul.* Should forget all my reverence for his knowledge, talents, learning — take him to my heart and love him — so firm, so conscientious, so *perfectly* true to his convictions. Had great power, great energy, great impulse, great self-control, great versatility, great concentrativeness. [*Question, "Is he fickle?"*] There are a great many ways of coming to the same end. Should you call the bee fickle, that went from flower to flower after honey? A man of *very large nature.* A great deal of caution, notwithstanding his apparent want of it. A very, singular, unusual compound. He is more universally developed than most persons, yet is not a *whole.* The various elements don't seem to me to be perfectly harmonized. Doesn't seem to have lived long enough for it. The work wasn't done when this letter was written at any rate. Calls to mind Mr. Channing's fountain in the palace, — the five, four, and three outer rooms in order, but the unitary stream from the central one not flowing out and binding all into a whole. Well — he'll have time enough to do it — he was *too busy, too active.* Do you think this concern for the race came thro' the reason or the heart? [*She was not answered.*] It seems to me thro' the reason. Thro' ignorance this person injured himself physically and morally. That seems a thing of the past, — yet its effects are wofully apparent. [*Question, "Was he confiding?"*] Both confiding and suspicious — confiding by nature — became suspicious by circumstances. He isn't living. In the latter part of his life was more confiding — a very different and higher state of confidingness than the first. It is pleasing to think of him as a boy — an honest heartedness about him — something of girlish delicacy and tenderness, — conscientiousness. Then there came the dark ages — seems as if he did wrong conscientiously. Seems as if he had a desire to know evil experimentally, therefore he did wrong. There must have been a horrible time in his life. Seems demoniacal, like ravening wolves, I don't think I can convey an impression of that time — perfectly fiendish. I can't convey the feeling of the actuality and unreality of it to me — don't seem that his heart had part in it. Seems to have acted vilely. Seems to have gone into it very thoroughly and yet with no reality. It was *devilishly cold.* He had a sort of fiendish delight in it too. Seems as if he put his better nature to sleep for a while — a gradual transition from his happy boyhood, which was so beautiful to think of — perhaps there was too much sensibility, a gentle, thoughtful boy. [*Laughing*] Should think he loved *rabbits.* Had a great love of justice: might have been thought irritable. Had rather think of him in his old age. There seems a greater harmony and blending in him than when this letter was written. He's more softened and purer — yet don't seem wholly pure.

It is frightful to think how ineradicable are the traces of sin. As I see him now, I see a great deal of purity and yet these dark lines. The purity is far greater than the stains. I've no words to tell it as I see it, seems to be a vision of the character. He seems to have plunged suddenly into sin, recklessly, not heartily — a fiendish joy.

Have not told you *anything* about him yet. He wished to know *everything* — felt you could not know anything unless you knew *everything*. I don't feel disposed to speak of him by particular traits. He was more intellectual than spiritual. [*She told me afterwards that the moment she said this Fourier came to her,* — *so mournful he looked almost reprovingly at her. She asked him, Isn't it so? and he acknowledged it.*] You talk of the ruling passion strong in death. It's strong *after* death with him. He is sadder now at this moment than he ever was when living. Sees his errors, sees the fearful consequences of them. I could almost attribute to him the vices of the most depraved — yet one of the *strongest* feelings in his nature is the love of justice. He felt that his work was not completed. He stays by, longing to see it done. Knows he was more intellectual than spiritual, and it is sadness to him now. The good is to him transparent. He dwells in the dark lines — you would not see it in one less good. He has great purity, devotedness, self-sacrificingness — errors of judgment and of conduct. I never knew before the danger of errors of judgment. I see how the wrong acts reacted on him, prevented his seeing clearly — lamed, warped, crippled him. Have I dwelt more on the errors than beauties of his character? Have not told you anything about him yet. I know a good deal about him. He never acted from one single motive, and yet you might say he always acted from one — love of truth. Had a great desire of knowledge — would give up everything to go where the truth would lead. So, in his desire to find, he went where it never could be found (these vices), into a bad atmosphere which affected his vision. So he could never see afterwards as he might have seen. A great love of completing his plans — grasped at the whole. When I speak of his love for the race, it is not so much a flowing love, yet at times I see that flowing, entrancing love. Seems rather a love of justice — sense of right. He could weep over the wrongs done to the race, and the next moment laugh at the saddest things. Has at times the confidingness of a little child. He had at times not a cold (that would do him injustice!) but a *warm*, calculating caution. Had a great love of figures and numbers — must have had because, if I think of colors and sounds, they arrange themselves in figures. Must have been a critic. [*Question, "Had he insight?"*] His *in*-sight was *out*sight. [*Question, "Was he mainly right in his views?"*] Not wholly right — not wrong. *A great deal more* right than wrong. Something clipped his wings; he could not fly as freely as he ought. Had a want of expansion, which sounds absurd. — There were limits set, when they should not have been — hadn't quite faith enough to leave the earth wholly — had *great* faith, *boundless* faith, *crazy* faith almost, yet didn't soar as he might. Had faith that what he *willed* would be done, — what he *wished* would be accomplished. Wasn't spiritual enough. I think there was a want within — was injured by those dark experiences — they hung like a heavy weight upon him. He is not free now, tho' much freer. He sees that they were errors — mourns them. Still he doesn't soar, — soars broad not high. A very difficult nature to speak of. In making any one, single statement I should do him injustice. [*Question, "His idea of God?"*] Do you think his own plans stand to him in the place of God? I can't tell. Should not like to say so. He was not irreligious — must *see* God in all — must *know* it, whether he felt it or not. A man I respect, mourn over, pity, (presumptuous as it seems) reverence and love — doesn't satisfy. He is *so much,* I can't help mourning that he is not all — one must be perfect in all to be perfect in anything. So these dark lines in the character make the purity less pure. What a joyous companion he must have been! *With him,* I should think I could move the world — that all things were possible. Should think that fiend went pretty much to sleep the last of his life. [*Question, "What form did the fiend take?"*] A sort of devilish maliciousness. Hatred of injustice might have led him to hate those that thwarted him.

CHARLES FOURIER

A Second Reading Sent to William H. Channing

Resolve — so decided that it is perfectly calm — seems to be solving a mathematical problem. Feeling of dignity and reserve — he is standing on his guard — also a hearty laugh inwardly as if at some one's shallowness — Great perseverances — energy of tho't and action — sadness — Justice has not been done him — he seems to have been injured by those he tho't friends. Great versatility. Sudden change of feeling — Scornful laugh — Feeling of indifference aroused by sense of injustice — I am continually thinking of the St. Simonians — They lose sight of vast and important principles — In fact they have no science — They have alighted on many great truths but their system is not a whole — They mean well but cannot succeed — God is necessary to any complete system — A knowledge of his method of operation — of his laws — one must begin at the very beginning — A complete change is necessary — It is not till the third generation of practical Associationists that you can expect much —

Indignation — a restrained feeling of impatient patience — a checked fire-brand — Power of words — One who could express strongly and clearly — Would be a light in dark places — Patient with the mass, impatient with the individual — Yet never weary of explaining — opening lights in all directions for one who received — Glad to see him in this light, so rich — so genial — such humor — such power of adapting himself to his hearers.

Mathematics — mathematics — mathematics — He attracts and enchants some by the poetry of his mathematics — He convinces others by the solid, undeniable prose — There's no escape from some of his arguments — His position is dignified — He demands nothing but that persons should use their reason — Should open their eyes to the light he sheds around them — There seems no tho't of self now — but an entire devotion to truth — Great quickness and clear sightedness — The husks fall off and things fall into their right places beneath his eyes — His patience peculiarly strikes me — Such activity and yet such restraining power — Such a waiting till all things are prepared. He would not risk the end thro' any unwise haste — His heart is very tender especially towards the young — to all the necessarily weak and dependent, tho' he despises imbecility — He loves little animals — Would be very considerate of those he loved — The tho't crosses my mind of doing some kind act for a sister. "This would give her pleasure." — I see a tall plant with rich, high-coloured blooms — the sister is in the country — He will send or carry this to her — "It would be so pleasant a surprise" —

He seems *materially* broad — He is brave — He does not repel — He gives himself freely to others, tho' this does not require any effort on his part — Experience has made him more cautious — more distant and doubting than he was by nature — He would have acquired Phonography rapidly and been much interested in it. A keen observer and inference-drawer — This he would do outwardly and mathematically. He would not see the motive in the act — but would deduce it from the act and that most accurately. He seems manly — he would bear attacks on himself with pride and patience — perhaps naturally hasty and irritable — Here all selfish considerations are lost — He is absorbed in great truth and elevated by it — How devotion to a great cause ennobles one — Scorn of the low — feeble — and cowardly — Unconquerable, patient energy — quite in earnest — Seems to be dwelling on some peculiar branch or division which he aims to set forth in a clear light and adapt to the vision of those to whom he presents it — Great quickness of thought, great desire for accuracy — Allegory — Allegorical — All nature teaches — every thing means something more than meets the outward eye — Each form has its signification — Nature teaches us, or would, in every way — Thro' the eye — the ear — the smell — the texture — the flavor — We shall not always eat so incoherently — but shall eat *musically* — harmoniously. No wonder that we live so antagonistically when we make ourselves the receptacle of such antagonist principles — How beautiful, how refined will this part of life become — One would enjoy the preparation of food (and *the devouring*) as one now enjoys painting — there will be that delight in blending harmoniously — in forming new combinations — in creating — in making a beautiful whole — Then indeed may we build up these bodies, to become fitting temples and wondrously beautiful will they be — It makes me shudder to think of our present savageness. This is a new pleasure and elevated life — life of the senses never seemed so attractive to me before — I grow elegant and refined in the tho't — I would have every motion, grace — every tone of music to satisfy me — I am surrounded by the most exquisitely harmonious arrangements — The fragrances around me are musically disposed — These miserable looking buildings, the abodes of bodies capable of such delights — I wonder that the earth does not reject them from her bosom — They encumber and disfigure it — I did not believe that the outward arrangements could have such power over one — I expand and would be large and noble and beautiful and graceful — that I may not be out of place — The perfection of the parts giving this perfect whole makes one long to be perfect inwardly and completely — Now I feel very sad — I look at Paris and groan in spirit — Can such things ever be? There is not life enough here to begin to build upon — Was that all a dream? No — It is God's truth and it must be so. That ever it has dawned on the mind of man is proof that it can be accomplished — It will be and angels will sing *Jubilate* — Even now the thick clouds are dispersing and the line of light shows itself in the *Western* sky and the East will yet reflect back its rays — Light travels swiftly — How beautiful becomes the earth in its beams — and this rainbow — thrice repeated — fills my soul with hope — with certainty — Never was there show of such promise — Behold a new Heaven and a new earth!

Now can I labor — keeping the end in sight and I cannot be discouraged, come what may — The dark shades of night are settling around me— I know — but the stars will enlighten it and the glorious morning will soon dawn. God speed the coming — No — It will come when the earth is ready — God strengthen and prepare us for it —

He has religious *feeling* — Is enthusiastic — Has a great deal of feeling — quick sympathies — I like his manner with his opponents — generally — He is willing to concede to them *all* that they can in justice claim — He can well afford to be generous — His views are so incontestably superior — they are founded on a rock — I like St. Simon's aspiration but his views seem like "the baseless fabric of a vision" — as if the solid earth in its revolvings would leave them floating in thin air, whilst Fourier's seem part and parcel of our good old mother — clinging tight to her bosom — There's a generous freeness in St. Simon which pleases me, but after all Fourier gives us the truest liberty.

THE AMERICAN UTOPIAN ADVENTURE

sources for the study of communitarian socialism in the United States 1680–1880

Series One

Edward D. Andrews THE COMMUNITY INDUSTRIES OF THE SHAKERS (1932)

Adin Ballou HISTORY OF THE HOPEDALE COMMUNITY from its inception to its virtual submergence in the Hopedale Parish. Edited by W. S. Heywood (1897)

Paul Brown TWELVE MONTHS IN NEW HARMONY presenting a faithful account of the principal occurrences that have taken place there during that period; interspersed with remarks (1827)

John S. Duss THE HARMONISTS. A personal history (1943)

Frederick W. Evans AUTOBIOGRAPHY OF A SHAKER and revelation of the Apocalypse. With an appendix. Enlarged edition (1888)

Parke Godwin A POPULAR VIEW OF THE DOCTRINES OF CHARLES FOURIER (1844) DEMOCRACY, CONSTRUCTIVE AND PACIFIC (1844)

Walter C. Klein JOHANN CONRAD BEISSEL, MYSTIC AND MARTINET, 1690–1768 (1942)

William J. McNiff HEAVEN ON EARTH: A PLANNED MORMON SOCIETY (1940) With "Communism among the Mormons," by Hamilton Gardner

Michael A. Mikkelsen THE BISHOP HILL COLONY. A religious, communistic settlement in Henry County, Illinois (1892) With "Eric Janson and the Bishop Hill Colony," by Silvert Erdahl

Oneida Community BIBLE COMMUNISM. A compilation from the annual reports and other publications of the Oneida Association and its branches, presenting, in connection with their history, a summary view of their religious and social theories (1853)

Marianne (Dwight) Orvis LETTERS FROM BROOK FARM 1841–1847. Edited by Amy L. Reed (1928)

Robert A. Parker A YANKEE SAINT. John Humphrey Noyes and the Oneida Community (1935)

A. J. G. Perkins & Thersa Wolfson FRANCES WRIGHT: FREE ENQUIRER. The study of a temperament (1939)

Jules Prudhommeaux ICARIE ET SON FONDATEUR, ÉTIENNE CABET. Contribution à l'étude du socialisme expérimental (1907)

Albert Shaw ICARIA. A chapter in the history of communism (1884)